Case studies in business

A skills-based approach

Sheila May

Pitman

PITMAN PUBLISHING LIMITED
128 Long Acre, London WC2E 9AN

Associated Companies
Pitman Publishing Pty Ltd, Melbourne
Pitman Publishing New Zealand Ltd, Wellington

© Sheila May 1984

British Library Cataloguing in Publication Data

May, Sheila
   Case studies in business.
   1. Business education—Great Britain
   2. Case method
   I. Title
   658'.00722   HF1141

First published in Great Britain 1984
Reprinted 1985

Printed in Great Britain at The Pitman Press, Bath

ISBN 0 273 01941 4

Contents

Preface

This book is about case studies and how to handle them successfully. Although addressed to the student it will also be of value to lecturers who are preparing students for courses using case studies as a teaching and examining method.

The use of cases in business studies has mushroomed in recent years. They form part of the teaching strategy in many courses and a number of examining boards now set case study examinations. As a consequence, many students pass through courses using cases, but do so without learning the problem solving and decision making *skills* which firstly are necessary for effective case study work and secondly can be transferred to solving real life problems.

This book is an attempt to remedy the situation. It aims both to help in courses where case studies are used and there is no instruction in the techniques, and to instruct those students studying alone. Lecturers will find that it can be used as the basis for courses leading up to a case study examination; for example, that of The Institute of Administrative Management. Alternatively, relevant parts of the book can be used in any course to teach problem solving techniques prior to embarking upon case study work.

These problem solving skills can be universally applied and the book will be useful in courses on clear thinking, how to study, and improving communications and human relationships. It will also serve as a guide to anyone who has to study a real life case which is to be the foundation for writing a project, as indicated in the following extract from the National Examinations Board for Supervisory Studies booklet 'Notes for Guidance on Projects'.

'Any exercise which you do, either alone or with the group, is a test of your ability to apply the knowledge you have gained to the practical solution of a problem. The project is a test therefore of your ability to observe and record information about a problem. Next it tests your ability to analyse that information; that is, to examine the facts of the matter in detail so that you really understand what it is all about. After you have collected and analysed your material you have to devise a solution to the problem and present it in a convincing way.

You may also be wondering about the relevance of a project to your work as a supervisor. The answer to that is quite simple. A project is an exercise in problem identification and solution and you, as a supervisor, will be doing those things all the time.'

This underlines a further value of the book – teaching problem solving skills which can be applied in the real world.

Part I introduces the techniques and skills necessary to tackle case studies. Each skill is analysed and exercises are given for practice.

Part 2 comprises cases from examining boards and a number of individual case writers; they may be used for practice. The choice of cases was partly determined by their largely non-technical nature. It should be possible, therefore, not only to isolate the problems and determine the causes in each case, but also to attempt a solution even if the subject is an unfamiliar one.

For higher level courses these cases should be supplemented with more complex ones and longer cases than is practicable to include in this book. Naturally, more technical cases should also be obtained and practised upon where relevant. Books of cases can be bought or borrowed and copies of past examination papers are available from examining boards.

Case studies play an invaluable role in stimulating thought and providing opportunities to gain insight into problems and into opposing views about those problems. This is only partially accomplished if they are not handled skilfully. It is the author's sincere hope that students and lecturers alike will find the learning/teaching process enhanced by a study of the techniques suggested in this book.

Acknowledgments

I am indebted to the organisations, examining boards and individual case writers who so willingly gave permission for the use of their cases, namely:

Daynes Electronics Company on page 9, copyright of which belongs to The Institute of Administrative Management.

Amfisbe Tools Ltd on page 22, copyright of which belongs to The Institution of Industrial Managers.

'The meter scheme', copyright of which rests with John L Heath, Leicester Polytechnic School of Management.

'A question of training', copyright of which rests with AIR Swabe.

'The distorting mirror', copyright of which rests with the Institute of Supervisory Management.

'The Bold House Hotel', copyright of which rests with the Institute of Marketing (used in Diploma in Marketing $1\frac{1}{2}$ hr unseen exam paper in Marketing Management – Planning and Control).

'Western Sausage Co Ltd', copyright of which rests with the National Examinations Board for Supervisory Studies (prepared by Kenneth E Roberts, Management Centre, North Staffordshire Polytechnic).

'Jenkinsons Ltd', copyright of which rests with P Laycock, City of Birmingham Polytechnic.

'Wearwell Footwear Ltd', copyright of which rests with the Royal Society of Arts (used in Office Supervisory Studies 2 hr unseen exam paper in Organisation and Techniques of Office Management [Compulsory Module]).

'Westborough Bus Company', copyright of which rests with the Institute of Administrative Management (used in Certificate in Administrative Management 3 hr unseen exam paper).

'Menlath Products', copyright of which rests with the Institution of Industrial Managers (used in 3 hr unseen external exam paper in Singapore).

'Victoria Printing Co Ltd', copyright of which rests with the National Examinations Board for Supervisory Studies (prepared by Kenneth E Roberts, Management Centre, North Staffordshire Polytechnic).

'A matter of choice', copyright of which rests with the Institute of Marketing (used in Diploma in Marketing $1\frac{1}{2}$ hr unseen exam paper in Marketing Management – Planning and Control).

'Jamesons Ltd', copyright of which rests with the Royal Society of Arts (used in Office Supervisory Studies 2 hr unseen exam paper in Communication Skills and Human Relations).

'Powa Drill Co Ltd', copyright of which rests with the London Chamber of Commerce and Industry (used in Private and Executive Secretary's Diploma exam in Management Appreciation).

I would like to record my thanks to the Luton College of Higher Education staff at Putteridge Bury, and in particular to Hugh McKay, for giving encouragement to my initial work undertaken while studying for the Diploma in Management Studies in 1979; to Ken Burgess, Chairman of the Institute of Administrative Management Case Study Working Party, who played a major role in the first publication of some of this material as an article in *The British Journal of Administrative Management*; to John Heath of the Executive Committee of The Case Clearing House; and Brian Howlett, chief examiner of the Institute of Administrative Management Certificate Case Study, who encouraged my subsequent development of this article into its present book form.

My thanks would be incomplete without an acknowledgment of the part my family have played by accepting that I have other responsibilities. For this reason I dedicate the book to my mother, my husband and my two sons Adam and Robin.

SM
1984

Part 1 Case study skills

1 Introducing cases

What attracted you to this book?

Was it because you are on a course which includes case studies and you want to learn how to handle them more skilfully?

Was it because you have to take a case study examination?

Was it because you want to know more about this method of learning?

If your reason is one of these or any other which requires that you be competent in handling cases then this book is addressed to you.

It aims to give a facility and ease with cases by suggesting a strategy for dealing with them: how to read for understanding, how to handle the information, how to set about the process of decision making and how to present your ideas. There is a chapter on case study examinations which outlines hints for success and warns against pitfalls to avoid. Finally, after a chapter pointing out that you must not expect case study work to be easy, you will find a description of the many benefits you might expect to gain.

Case study is a means of learning in which you must actively participate. Do not be content therefore merely to read the book. Be prepared to work on the skill development suggestions indicated in the chapters and work through the cases which you will find in Part 2. But first let us look at what cases are, why they are used and how you might encounter them.

What is a case?

A case is basically an account of problem situations and events in a real or an imagined organisation. Some describe the unsuccessful handling of such situations by the characters portrayed and these will provide you with an opportunity for critical analysis and the developing of more effective measures. Some will require you to identify an underlying issue in a complex situation and then suggest how this might be dealt with. Others call for a choice to be made between alternative courses of action which of necessity means that you also have to predict their outcomes.

You are likely to find case study work exciting, irritating, amusing, depressing, rewarding, punishing, intriguing and more. The feelings invoked, the experience gained and the opportunities presented are as many and as varied as the cases themselves since these attempt to simulate real life situations, which like life are multi-faceted.

Cases may be short or long, simple or complex, and contain a single issue or embody a number. Their one common factor is that they provide a means for analysing data, identifying problems and decision making. These are the characteristics that distinguish a real problem solving case from others which might be called cases but are in effect merely storylines upon which to base traditional questions with 'right' answers. Cases do not always have right answers as will be explained later.

This does not mean that questions may not be posed on real cases. They often are, especially on examination cases. Many are also written such that anyone handling them is led to apply certain techniques and knowledge. It is the need for the techniques and knowledge to be applied to decision making, as opposed to being written about theoretically, that is the important distinction.

Ideas for handling cases may come from a textbook but do not give complete answers. If you can open a textbook and copy out a case 'answer' word for word then strictly speaking you are not handling a real problem case.

A case can take many forms; and film, video, audio and tape/slide formats are sometimes used to give a sense of realism. Mainly for reasons of cost, speed and convenience, however, the written case is the type you are likely to encounter most often.

Why are cases used?

When cases were first introduced into business education at Harvard early this century their use in this field was an innovation. Traditionally, studying cases was a technique used in schools of law and medicine but it came to be realised at the School of Business Administration that:

a Business is similar to law in that there is a great deal of working knowledge not specifically laid down.

b Business is similar to medicine in that the problems presented are often not the true ones. As an example, a doctor will listen to a patient relaying his symptoms but may then have to question him closely in order to discover the real reason why that person has come to see him. Similarly, businessmen often find, after spending much time and effort trying to resolve a problem, that something else is causing the trouble!

The business studies student must endeavour to develop the interpretive and communicating skills of the law student, the reasoning and diagnostic skills of the medical student and the decision making skills of both. It therefore seemed a reasonable assumption that a proven method of study for law and medicine would be equally useful for the study of business. Experience has indeed shown this to be so with the result that cases are now used in business education both to aid learning and as a means of assessment.

An additional benefit, much needed because of the diversity of business knowledge, is that cases promote the taking of an overall view and thus break down rigid subject barriers. Since life is not neatly packaged into subjects, in any one situation you might be called upon to apply any part of your knowledge and use any of your skills. An essential difference between knowledge and skills is that you can learn knowledge but skills require practice. This is a major justification for the use of cases since handling them enables you to practise the skills of:

- problem identification
- data handling
- decision making
- analytical and critical thinking
- attitude training
- interpersonal relationships
- communication
- judgment making
- handling assumption and inference

How might you meet cases?

You are likely to encounter cases on a course. Lecturers use cases in a variety of ways, for example:

a The case is issued to each student with a request that it be studied prior to a class discussion.
b As a, but class discussion commences immediately. This is to simulate the real life situation where a problem has to be dealt with on the spot.
c As a or b, but with discussion in small groups. Each group is required to analyse the case and report back to the whole class.
d The case is handed out with a request that an analysis be written and handed in at a later date.
e As d, but the write-up has to be done immediately, possibly under examination conditions. This is in preparation for the type of case study examination where the case is not seen beforehand.
f The case is in audio/visual form. This might be played straight through or stopped at appropriate places for a discussion of what has already taken place or for a prediction of the outcome.
g Only part of the information is given out with further data available upon request. This is a variation intended to develop the skill of asking

the right questions. Only those who do so receive the information needed to solve the case problems!

h The case is built around role play. Each player is given an outline of the role he is to assume. Since the outcome is not predetermined, but depends upon how each player develops the role, this enables people to 'feel' the events and have some control over developments. The case, as role played, is used for later analysis.

A lecturer might precede any of these methods by talking about the principles involved in the case or interject mini lectures at appropriate places in the discussion. Use of the case is then a valuable aid to the retention of that knowledge because it gives immediate practice in applying it.

Where are cases used?

Cases have been most widely used in various aspects of management training. This is because they provide what is of obvious benefit to managers – opportunities to practise and develop both analytical skills and the ability to apply judgment.

What has been less obvious previously, but is now receiving greater recognition as a result of the accelerated speed of technological advance, is that the use of these skills is often required lower down the responsibility ladder. Unusual and previously unencountered situations are faced frequently by people at all levels in their everyday working lives. As a result, career prospects in many fields are bound up with the ability to make right decisions at the right time and for the right reasons, and employers are now looking for this ability.

This wider appreciation of increased demands upon people coupled with an acknowledgment of the value of case studies in training for decision making has resulted in cases being introduced into a greater variety of courses. In addition, examining boards are turning to 'the case' as a means of assessing candidates' potential capabilities for dealing with real life problems. Thus the use of cases is growing and becoming a familiar study and examination feature for many people.

From this has arisen the need to view both teaching and learning in a new light. The traditional learning of answers does not apply to cases because there are no 'answers' to learn. What has to be learnt instead are problem solving techniques which can be practised and turned into skills.

Why do you need skills?

When you work on a case you do so with a unique set of experiences, attitudes, knowledge and opinion resulting from years of being exposed to influences different from those affecting other people. Consequently, the alternative solutions you derive for a case, the criteria you use to evaluate them and the final recommendations you make are likely to vary significantly from those made by anyone else. This is the reason why there cannot be just one correct 'answer' to a case problem.

Working on a case requires your accumulated knowledge and experience combined with learnt and developed case analysis skills. The techniques for acquiring these skills can be found in this book. They will give you a framework to use when faced with what might otherwise appear to be an unstructured and daunting task – resolving a case or real life problem situation.

2 Studying cases

How to begin?

First, accept that there can be no one magic formula because the situations and the problems presented in cases are infinitely variable. The key to success lies in learning and applying a series of guidelines and checklists which will enable you to work on a case logically and with confidence. These guidelines cover:

- understanding the case situation
- identifying and defining the problems
- creating and developing alternative approaches to solving the problems
- predicting the outcomes of the alternatives
- evaluating and deciding upon the most favourable course of action
- communicating the results of your work

In the chapters that follow you will find detailed information on these guidelines and opportunities for applying the techniques suggested. In this chapter you will learn how to apply the guidelines for 'understanding the case situation'.

Gain an overall impression

When you first receive a case you are likely to be keen to know what it is all about. Satisfy your curiosity. Read through the case quickly without stopping to re-read anything not immediately clear or evaluating any aspect. From this you should expect to obtain a general picture of the overall situation and discover who the characters are.

Skill development

Read through the following case quickly as suggested:

Daynes Electronics Company

The Daynes Electronics Company started as a small organisation interested in integrated circuits. Over the past 10 years the company has expanded steadily and has recently received some large orders for TV games. The office expansion that has taken place has been under three managers each of whom is in charge of one of the functions of production, distribution and finance. No single person has been in charge of the office services.

Each functional manager maintains his own filing, typing, mailing and duplication departments. Supervisors are in charge of the functional activities under the headings of production, distribution and finance. Part of the organisation chart indicates that under production there are supervisors in charge of purchasing, receiving, storing, accounts payable, factory payroll, cost accounting and shipping. Under the heading of distribution there are supervisors in charge of sales, advertising, credit and accounts receivable. Under the direction of the manager in charge of finance there are supervisors for financial accounting, taxes, government reports and returns and office payrolls. The total office staff consists of 160 people.

Many of these supervisors have been shifted into their positions with little knowledge of systems or methods. The supervisors are hard pressed to get the work done because of inefficiency, lack of knowledge and needless duplication of records and work. Office equipment has been ordered from time to time and placed where it was thought it would be used later.

The general manager of the company, Mr Mike Davey, feels frustrated by the fact that whenever he wants information he must go to several sources and waste time in locating it. He has also noticed the amount of idle equipment in the offices and the delay in the preparation of certain operating reports.

Mr Davey has recently had a conference with the three managers in charge of production, finance and distribution activities and indicated his dissatisfaction. The production manager, the marketing manager and the treasurer all feel that none of them can give up or change any of their work routines or present personnel.

Mr Davey feels that something must be done in the interests of a more efficient organisation and lower costs. He has called upon you to find out how it might be possible to reorganise the office services so that a better utilisation of present personnel and equipment might achieve the objectives of greater and faster output, and reduced costs.

What overall impression have you gained from this first reading?

1   Is the company well organised with clearly defined responsibilities for each manager?
2   Are the responsibilities of each manager in accord with his function?
3   Has the company developed in an *ad hoc* manner?
4   Has there been an efficient utilisation of resources?

Self check

From your reading you should have gained an overall impression of Daynes Electronics as a company which has developed in an *ad hoc* manner. This lack of planning is shown in a mixing up of functional activities; for example, some of the finance functions are dealt with by the production and distribution departments. This has in turn led to duplicated and unused resources.

Understand what is required

You cannot handle a case adequately unless you know exactly what is required. Are you being asked:

a   'to do' or 'to advise'?
b   to look at the whole case or only at certain aspects of it?
c   to assume the role of one of the characters?
d   to present your findings in a specific manner?

The instructions given with the Daynes case were in the form of questions:

1   Prepare a chart showing the current organisation and another chart indicating the changes you would make in the organisation structure. Write brief notes justifying the changes.
2   Discuss the possibility of centralised services in this organisation.
3   How would you attempt to rationalise the situation for individual personnel?
4   Give details of a suitable executive training programme in this situation.

5 How would you approach the problem of improving office layout, deciding on the office equipment which is needed and what is currently available in the offices?

(All questions carry equal marks)

Note the mode of presentation required for each question. It is helpful to underline these; for example, prepare a chart, brief notes.

Make sure you understand exactly what is meant by terms such as 'discuss'. In connection with this, you will find it an advantage to be familiar with the list of key verbs (see Appendix). Study this; it might prevent you from answering an examination question incorrectly.

Be alert to the wording of questions in every respect. The use of the expression 'How would you', for example, means that you should answer the question in a practical manner and is an indication that what will be looked for are your own ideas.

The final note 'All questions carry equal marks' is not only for information but is advice to spend approximately the same amount of time on each question. It is advice which should be heeded. Do not get absorbed and spend too much time answering a question you can do well because this will cut down your time for answering those which might require greater thought. The extra time spent on any question is unlikely to yield many more marks and may endanger your finishing the paper. When time runs out for a question, jot down in note form whatever else you have to add and move on. Incidentally, the time allowance for Daynes Electronics, which was an examination case, was three hours.

Sometimes instructions are implied and 'hidden' in the narrative. Did you pick up from reading Daynes that the implied role to adopt is a consultancy one? Note the wording 'He has called upon you to find out . . .' There is nothing to indicate whether you are an employee of the company or an outside consultant but clearly you should adopt the role of 'expert'. In a later chapter you will read more of the importance of thinking yourself into a role but briefly this directs your thoughts and helps to keep ideas practical.

Before presenting your case commentary, whatever form this might take, it is as well to state what role you have adopted. Your reader or listener will then be able to follow your line of reasoning more readily.

Skill development

Look back at the Daynes Electronics case questions. Using the suggestions given after these and the Appendix key verbs list determine exactly what information is required and how the answer to each question is to be presented.

Isolate key information

To help you gain understanding of a case and pick out information in later stages of handling it you will find it useful to:

a Make notes in the margin as they occur to you, including points of theory.
b Underline key phrases which give clues as to how a particular situation/problem is developing.
c Use a lettering or numbering system to indicate any items which are linked.
d Number every tenth line in order to make future reference easy, for yourself when in discussion and to use for identifying specific items in a written presentation.

An alternative to *b* and *c* is to use the type of felt-tip pen which is fluorescent and sold for 'highlighting' passages in a text. A set of such pens in different colours is even better. Each colour can be used to highlight a certain category of information, for example, all that relating to one person, or all of the financial information. This provides a means of grouping information without having to write it all out, and has the added advantage of keeping it in context. But take care, do not get carried away and end up by highlighting everything!

Skill development

Go back over the Daynes case, this time applying instructions *a* to *d* just mentioned.

Read for understanding

The next stage is to read the case through at a much slower, thoughtful rate. Do not, however, jump to conclusions about the problems or try to solve them in any respect. Just aim for understanding, an awareness of the decisions to be made and of what is likely to influence them, such as the constraints and resources.

If you experience difficulties, an appreciation of the situation in the context of earlier developments, current trends and issues will help you to understand the problems. This can be gained from posing such questions as the following:

1. How have these affected what is going on?
2. What are the strengths and weaknesses of both the people and the organisation?
3. Are there underlying or long standing problems or difficulties?
4. Do opportunities for improvement exist? If so, where?
5. Where have there been gains or losses?
6. What was the effect of any decisions made?
7. What was the foundation for making them?
8. What are the facts, what assumptions and inferences made, what opinions stated, and what feelings and thoughts expressed?
9. What is the size of the problem?
10. Where did misunderstanding creep in?
11. What actually happened?

One factor to appreciate is the convention of writing cases in the past tense. A reason for this is so that an appropriate date can be used for the situation outlined; for example, 'In January 1983 Mr Sharples was appointed to the post of senior sales representative for the Home Counties'. This dating of a case may be arbitrary or for a particular reason – and this is where it can be a useful clue. Well known external events such as a period of high unemployment or a war might have a bearing upon the case situation and the significance of any dates given should therefore be considered.

Not only should you read in order to gain knowledge about the behaviour reported and to isolate the problems but also read in order to determine how the problems arose. Each sentence must be considered firstly for surface information and again for insight: look carefully at the words; search for leads; check if anything has been leading towards the present situation.

In many instances, clues can be found if you look for them in the narrative. Comments such as 'continued to disregard warnings', 'attempts made in vain' or 'again refused' indicate a long standing problem with the possibility of entrenched attitudes among the case characters. Indications of likely problems in relationships or leadership styles should be apparent when words and phrases such as 'supposed to be', 'ordered', 'generally expected', 'had not realised', 'was not happy', 'private discussions' and so on are used. These are not only a good indication of people's past behaviour but are also a clue as to how you might expect them to behave in the new situation brought about by your case solution. You must take the anticipated reactions of the case characters into consideration in your resolution of the case problems and so need to glean all the information you can about them.

Skill development

Now re-read the Daynes Electronics case (page 9), questioning each piece of information given. Determine what has led up to the present problems, whether or not new problems might arise and if so why you anticipate this.

Self check

Did you pick out the information showing a lead up to the present problems?: 'No single person has been in charge of office services', '. . . little knowledge of systems or methods', '. . . hard pressed to get the work done', '. . . inefficiency, lack of knowledge and needless duplication' and references to waste of time, idle equipment and delay?

It is equally important to recognise where problems might arise in implementing the recommendations you will be making at a later stage. Did you recognise the new problem likely to arise at Daynes? This lies in the attitudes towards change on the part of the three functional managers. In suggesting a course of action intended to resolve the problems, it will be necessary for you to suggest means of overcoming this resistance. No plans will succeed unless the managers can be persuaded to cooperate in the implementation of them.

Appraise facts and opinions

A thorough sifting of the information is the next task in case analysis. Unnecessary items, especially opinion and conjecture, are often included in the narratives, and picking out the relevant pieces of information while discarding those that confuse an issue is a key skill.

Always try to assess the likely attitudes and reactions of the characters in a case. What is plausible among the stated opinions? What has real bearing on the case? What can be put down to prejudice and bias?

Opinions are frequently reported in the form of a quotation or of a statement such as 'The supervisor believed that the increased output was a direct result of changes she had made'. Clearly, it is necessary to decide how valid such a statement is since this will have a bearing on your subsequent decision making.

Whatever your conclusions do not discount such statements. People's opinions influence their actions. If the supervisor does believe she has increased output, her future actions will be affected by that belief. This could mean that she might initiate similar changes at some future time and be undeterred by opposition.

Another type of information given in cases is financial data which, especially when it appears in the form of balance sheets and trading accounts, appears authoritative. Although such data cannot be disputed as fact nevertheless it is wise to question how the figures were arrived at – much as one would do in real life.

The valuation of stock is an example of a figure one should query. It is important to know how this was arrived at because accounting practices differ. A bias in favour of valuation at the lower of cost or market value means that in an inflationary period the stock is actually worth more than the amount stated. Your knowledge of this could influence your decisions and hence the need to establish the basis for such data. If it is not possible to do this, then it might be necessary to make an assumption. If you do so, be sure to state clearly what your assumption is otherwise the reader/examiner may not follow your reasoning.

Skill development

It states in the Daynes case that 'The supervisors are hard pressed to get the work done because of inefficiency, lack of knowledge and needless duplication of records and work'. Is this fact or opinion? What was the basis for your decision on this? Did you make an assumption?

It further states 'The production manager, the marketing manager and the treasurer all feel that none of them can give up or change any of their work routines or present personnel'. What bearing does this have on the case? How might it affect the implementation of suggestions put forward for reorganisation of the office?

Cultivate a questioning frame of mind

In dealing with case problems it is necessary to appreciate that there are constraints that are not present in real life. One is that it is not possible to make on-the-spot judgments. There is only the information provided by the case writer and the personnel involved cannot be questioned. Arising from this also is the fact that you are dependent upon the writer for the quality of the evidence. Some of this will be beyond doubt but even facts should be considered critically.

Skill development

Would you question any statement in the Daynes case?

Self check

You should!
   It is stated that the company has expanded steadily over the past 10 years. But to what extent? Large orders for TV games have been received recently. How large is large? Did you wonder about the comment that Mr Davey 'has also noticed the amount of idle equipment in the offices'. Questions such as 'Was that just chance?', 'How frequently does he pass by the equipment?' and 'When?' should be considered even though you cannot actually pose them to the people concerned. After having considered the rest of the evidence in the case, you might decide that the equipment really is lying idle but do not accept statements at their face value. Weigh them up in the light of other evidence.

Evaluate case facts

The same value cannot be placed upon all case 'facts'. Establish which are precise, which imprecise and which you have doubts about. The degree of precision is important at a later stage. This is when you have to choose between possible alternative courses of action. At that time, one of the considerations must be how much you can rely on the information upon which the possible courses of action have been based.

   In studying a case, the onus is on you to judge the validity or otherwise of every given piece of information. Adopt a questioning frame of mind, remembering that some of the information may have been included deliberately in order to test how adequately you are able to assess it!

Skill development

The skills we have discussed in this chapter are:

* gaining an overall impression
* understanding what is required
* isolating key information
* reading for understanding

- appraising facts and opinions
- cultivating a questioning frame of mind

Prepare a draft analysis of the following case, using this list of skills as pointers.

Kilmaine Stationery Supply Co Ltd

Kilmaine Stationery Supply Co Ltd is a major supplier of commercial stationery, office equipment, business machines and drawing office supplies. It markets much of its goods through specialist representatives and offers a free delivery service throughout the region. In order to keep the representatives on the road and ensure that the goods are delivered by the dates promised, the company maintains a fleet of cars and delivery vans. The person responsible for the fleet, its maintenance and the delivery of goods, is the distribution manager, a post for which you have been designated.

The current holder of the post, Mr Robertson, is due to retire in two months time in line with the company's 'retirement at 60' rule. Rumour has it that he does not want to go and asked (in vain) if he could stay on. Certainly, he shows no signs of relinquishing the reins even though you are to commence work in the department immediately in order to become familiar with its work. Mr Robertson's performance has apparently been poor for some time. He has always been disinclined to delegate or set up clear lines of communication and this has become a problem increasingly as his retirement has drawn nearer. Morale is at an all time low but this has not resulted in people leaving.

The previously phased replacement of vehicles has been allowed to slip and consequently a large proportion will need to be replaced within a short period of time. Maintenance contracts have been renewed without close scrutiny or shopping around and a number will require delicate re-negotiation.

Your previous post was as a senior sales representative and you are therefore familiar with that side of the business. You have a nodding acquaintance with the distribution office staff but do not know the drivers. You have no previous experience of fleet control or maintenance and clearly are unlikely to get much help from Mr Robertson who appears unwilling to accept your presence as his successor.

1 How can you most usefully spend the time until Mr Robertson leaves?
2 What will be your priorities when you assume control of distribution?
3 What problems do you anticipate in your first three months in the post?

3 Identifying and defining problems

Having examined the position as it exists in a case the next step is to isolate the problems in order to be able to suggest means of improving the situation. Unless the problems are correctly specified, your subsequent decision making might alleviate but cannot resolve the difficulties. An aid to this stage of analysis is to take the situation apart and then put it together again in a more convenient form.

Classify the information

Classifying the information will help. By rearranging the information under suitable headings, you are better placed to explore how facts and relationships interact, particularly in a complex case. The time this takes will vary from case to case but it is time well spent. You should not only then be more familiar with the case, but be able to identify individual issues more readily.

There are many ways of proceeding, but in general the more detailed the case the more structured the analysis needs to be. A method such as the following can be simplified or made more complex to suit the case:

a   List the characters. Not only their names and other information given, but what can be gleaned such as their attitudes and characteristics, relationships with others, responsibilities and the statements attributed to them.

  Ask yourself – 'Can I visualise these people?' This will help you to find out information about them which is not immediately obvious.

b   Note down what is known about the organisation:
  • what work is carried on
  • where the areas of conflict lie
  • the predominent management style
  • the communications
  • the facilities
  • the strength of the financial situation
  • whether or not there is a strong informal organisation underlying the formal

c   Chart the sequence of events in the case.

Train yourself to associate case and real life situations. When faced with a case problem, always consider if anything similar is happening in an organisation with which you are familiar. If so, what is being done to deal with it. Could this be applied to your case problem? Conversely, does it indicate how not to deal with the situation!

Skill development

Practise this by classifying as far as possible the whole or part of your own work organisation or another with which you are familiar. (See points *a* and *b* opposite.)

Identify the problems

After classifying the information, you should be very familiar with any case with which you are working and be aware of the obvious problems. However, not all problems are obvious, so in order not to miss any:

a List all those which you have so far identified.
b Consider if any are connected. They rarely come singly; either there are a number of problems interconnected or one is the cause of another.
c Determine if the problems so far listed are the real ones or only symptoms of others deeper rooted.
d Use your judgment on the statements made in the case. Could anything in these constitute problem areas?
e Check through the rest of your work on the course, and the syllabus, since you should expect the case to be related to these. By doing so you might realise that there are other problems which you had overlooked.

Specify the problems

If your analysis is sound and the problems have been precisely described then this provides a firm basis for deciding what can be done to resolve them. It is worthwhile, therefore, to take the time to write out a statement of the problems at this stage even if you feel that in your mind they are already completely specified. It will throw up any errors or inconsistencies and, because you have to think the situation through in order to set it down, does make sure that you have examined it thoroughly. Later, when working on your presentation it will be necessary to make such a statement, so you may as well derive the benefits sooner rather than later.

A correct definition of the problem is recognised as being such a vital element in decision making that if this has been well thought through and is clearly set down it should go a long way towards gaining a good grade in any case study assessment.

Determine the causes

Determining causes is an important stage which is not always given sufficient attention. Problems cannot be considered as solved unless their causes have been dealt with effectively.

In the short term it might be expedient to introduce what should only be looked upon as a first aid measure because untreated causes leave the way open for the problems to return. Long-term measures frequently require greater attention and in order to give this the root causes must be determined.

Sometimes, establishing the causes of problems requires a considerable amount of information sifting. If you do experience difficulty, search for links between the pieces of information:

- look for cause and effect
- consider symptoms

Think about relationships, those between events as well as those between people.

Pose questions such as 'What actually happened?', 'What is important?' and 'How did the misunderstanding arise?'

If you still cannot isolate the cause of a particular problem readily, try listing all the likely causes and then eliminate any which do not fit the circumstances. This will have led you to think widely and from the list of plausible causes with which you are left it should be possible to make a final choice.

Skill development

Read the Kilmaine case again (page 17) or apply what you have learnt so far to a work, college or personal problem situation. Identify the problems, making sure that they are the real ones, and determine the causes – the root ones.

Avoid pitfalls

It is very easy to associate similar factors and to assume that they have only one cause.

If it were stated in a case, for example, that there had been a change in procedures or management and it were also stated that labour turnover had increased, these could be interpreted as being connected. Indeed they might be, but not necessarily so. Each factor should be looked at carefully. If an incorrect connection is made, it can confuse and obscure the separate problems and so cover up the need to find separate causes and do something about them.

Nevertheless, be alert to relationships. If two events have coincided, as in the above example, then a possible connection should be investigated. Think of it as the putting together of a jigsaw puzzle – you find a piece which might fit, but suspend judgment until you have placed it in position and are then absolutely sure.

A pitfall to be avoided is closing your options. This can happen if you pinpoint the issues before exploring the situation thoroughly. If a too definite view of what is involved is adopted then this defines the scope and direction of thinking from then on. In effect, the parameters have been set. Important aspects may have been overlooked and it is wisest to defer further considerations until you have, with certainty, understood the problems.

You can also close your options by rushing to suggest answers, because in so doing you will have to evaluate your ideas too soon. You may then reject some as being unrealistic or defective in some other way. Although your first impressions may be correct, what you reject out of hand could carry the germ of a good solution, or given consideration serve to trigger off better ideas. Note down your thoughts as they occur to you but leave them at that. Always avoid seizing upon what appears to be a perfect answer. This inhibits further thought because one easily becomes attached to such 'inspirations' and is reluctant to consider other possibilities.

Skill development

Now try to put the ideas in this chapter into use in analysing the following case. Remember to:

- classify the information
- identify and specify the problems
- determine the causes
- avoid the pitfalls

Amfisbe Tools Ltd

Amfisbe Tools Ltd manufactures and distributes a range of garden and domestic tools. Part of its production is in metal goods but increasingly these are being replaced by plastic materials either in whole or in part. Its sales are through normal distribution channels though it does have a significant contract (some 20 per cent of output) with one of the nationwide stores which demands high conformity with its own specification and distinctive labelling and packaging.

The current recession has caused the management to take precautionary measures to meet further anticipated falls in demand which have been accommodated so far by working less overtime and reducing the proportion of 'bought in' components and parts wherever possible. During the last two months, a survey of both production and despatch departments has been undertaken to discover whether any sections have unduly high cost figures or significant room for economy. It has been noticed, particularly in the assembly shop, that financial control has been difficult, not least because of constantly changing flows of work and in some cases because of minor departures from specification in manufacture which have made assembly more difficult than anticipated. Most of the actual assembly operations are fairly simple involving mechanical fastening procedures, the use of a variety of adhesives and in some cases spot-welding. The assembly shop employs 45 people (30 men, 15 women). The assembly shop supervisor, George Brent, reports directly to the production manager, Tom Wilson, and he has three foremen reporting to him – Bill Harris (52), Jos Wilkins (41) and Cliff Ferguson (64).

Amfisbe Tools Ltd has some 85 per cent of shop floor workers unionised (TGWU and AUEW particularly). The shop steward in the assembly shop is Ivor Perkins (26), an energetic but unusual semi-skilled worker, who having started studying for chemistry 'A' levels left school before completion of his course. He has continued to be fascinated by the subject and has become the shop floor (and sometimes management) adhesives 'expert'. His general intelligence is respected by most of the shop floor males and a certain 'charm' does not go unnoticed by some of the women workers. He stands up firmly for workers' 'rights' and is gaining the reputation of being difficult by both his trade union local representatives and by management.

Workers in the assembly shop have usually felt themselves looked down upon since they were classed as unskilled or semi-skilled. Their work is largely repetitive and though on occasion (through overtime or favourable piece-rates) their wages match those in the production shops, their take-home pay is usually about 85 per cent of the factory average. Pressure has frequently been put on the assembly shop to increase productivity. George Brent has been encouraged to seek new and improved methods of assembly and to consider how appropriate training (or jigging) could help.

He has sometimes complained there has not been the investment necessary to achieve high output and that his recommendations to achieve a happy work force are ignored. Recently, for example, during a spell of very warm weather one assembly line (women) asked for fans, both to dispel varnish smells and to cool their working area. Wilson had looked into the matter but since no Factory Act requirements could actually be seen to have been contravened in this particular instance and fume extraction already appeared to meet regulative requirements he declined to authorise the necessary expenditure – some £600. On another occasion some of the male workers asked for more comfortable stools, ie of adjustable height, but again Brent had been unsuccessful in persuading Wilson.

The supervision of the assembly shop was divided by product. Harris looked after garden tool assembly, Wilkins after batch tools and Ferguson DIY products. In practice, assembly lines and groups were decided on a day-by-day basis according to the product mix and production schedule demands. This practice led to frequent changes of work groups though not necessarily of the actual kind of work undertaken. The 'stickers' (ie those using adhesive), for example, tended to keep to a certain area of the workshop and to keep to the job they did since successful 'stickers' tended to develop 'knacks' (skills) which were quite personal. However, from time to time preferences and capacities had to be overridden to keep assembly going.

Tom Wilson has come to the conclusion that the opportunity now occurs for significant reorganisation in the assembly shop. Cliff Ferguson retires at Christmas; three of the women assemblers are pregnant and two of the men are due to retire in the coming six months. Demand for the company's product is forecast as 20 per cent down for the first six months of next year. Ivor Perkins has stated that the assemblers will not cooperate with any reorganisation; they will not tolerate changes unless their wages are brought up to be in line with the rest of the plant. Brent has suggested that Perkins should be upgraded to supervisor but Wilson has argued that with the decline of output the shop will be oversupervised and that in any case if the shop were better organised less supervision would be necessary.

The position now is that Brent and Wilson have an icy relationship. Harris tends to agree with Brent while Wilkins feels the assembly shop both could and should be reorganised. He is a near neighbour of Perkins, who he finds friendly – they share a common interest in a local Scout Group.

4 Problem solving

We now move to the heart of the task. Do not be tempted to cut out the steps previously suggested, they are a necessary preliminary. Even a simple case needs to be thoroughly analysed, but obviously if it really is simple the analysis does not take too long. Beware of taking length as an indication of the complexity or otherwise of a case. Short ones are sometimes the most difficult to solve because there seems so little to get to grips with.

Set objectives

In setting objectives you are stating what you judge to be the desired state of affairs in the future. These objectives should be described in terms of the effects which the case characters can influence, and ought to provide positive guidelines. You can determine them by considering questions such as:

1 What is to be accomplished?
2 What problems are to be corrected?
3 What situations need to be improved?
4 Where are we trying to go?
5 What results should be expected?
6 What do we want to minimise/maximise?

When dealing with each question remember that you may be setting short and/or long term objectives.

In formulating objectives, you should be seeking to achieve the most advantageous return from the use of the resources available. Basically, these fall into the 'three M categories' – manpower, materials and machines. In general, difficulties arise because the availability of each resource is limited. There is usually a need to consider what must be conserved or utilised, minimised or maximised. Sometimes it is necessary to weigh up matters of greatest importance against important but less essential matters since not all may be attainable. Deciding priorities is not easy. If you experience difficulty here, try ranking the objectives in order of importance and this should help to direct your thinking.

Skill development

Practise setting objectives by applying questions 1 to 6 to some aspect of the organisation in which you work, or to the Daynes case (page 9).

Create and develop alternative approaches

In many respects, this stage is rather different from the foregoing which have required a predominantly logical approach. This is the stage of creating ideas where techniques alone will not work. You should seek to produce a number of alternatives for resolving the problems – not too many to confuse but sufficient to give a real choice.

In order to get ideas flowing consider:

a the opportunities available.
b the threats, ie what could prevent the opportunities being taken.
c the strengths and weaknesses of the organisation.

This helps to clarify what short term measures and long term plans have to be formulated. Remember that short term measures are primarily to achieve immediate results. Long term plans should minimise weaknesses and threats whilst reinforcing strengths and maximising opportunities.

You will find it helpful to pose a sequence of questions such as:

1 What are the negative factors?
2 What are the positive factors?
3 How can 1 be minimised and 2 be maximised?
4 Are individuals pulling their weight?
5 Are resources being utilised to best advantage?
6 If the answer to either 4 or 5 is no – why not?
7 What can be done to overcome this?
8 What is the least degree of reorganisation necessary for solving the problem?

In the short term, when it is a matter of getting immediate problems resolved in order to keep some system, machine, etc operational or to ease a human relations problem, 8 is of prime importance. In the long term it may of course be necessary to take more radical measures in order to prevent the problems reappearing.

You will probably already be aware that ideas on resolving a problem frequently occur when your mind is not actively directed towards it. There seem to be two main reasons for this. First, your way of looking at the problem may have become fixed, and taking the pressure off allows a new perspective to develop. Second, the mind appears to carry on solving problems while you are not consciously doing so. Consequently, if you take a break from working on a case ideas might well flow more readily when it is taken up again.

If time does not allow for such a break, as in an examination for instance, then letting ideas flow without specifically directing them may bring forth new ones.

More concretely, when able to do so, research any sources where help may be available. Do not forget yourself as a resource. Apply your own knowledge and past experience. Think through the theory learnt on your course. Read through the syllabus. These might act as triggers.

Skill development

Think of as many alternative approaches as you can to resolving the problems at Amfisbe (page 22).

Personalise the problem

At this point, it is worth mentioning the benefits if you are willing to reach out towards the circumstances of the case with imagination and empathy. This cannot be emphasised too strongly. The more you are able to enter into the quandary of the case decision maker the more the question becomes 'What would I do?' This personalising of a problem generally leads to the finding of a solution because if it really were your problem you would have no option but to find one! More than that the solution is likely to be a practical one since it would be your responsibility to implement it.

This personalising may also help you later when working on the case presentation. Frequently, an instruction will state that the role of a character in the case has to be adopted. This means that the presentation has to be written as though from that person. Obviously, the earlier the role is accepted the more in character will be your handling of the situation. Adopting a role also helps you to concentrate more specifically upon a problem and thus avoid making vague recommendations.

Skill development

Practice the personalising of problems by trying to think of ideas for resolving any with which you are familiar in real life. Avoid your own problems. Consider someone else's and put yourself in their shoes. Think widely but do not attempt at this stage to evaluate your ideas or reach any decisions.

Use deduction, inference and assumption

Deduction, inference and assumption are valuable aids to reasoning if treated with caution, if the differences between them is appreciated and if they are used correctly.

A **deduction** is a specific conclusion drawn from a general fact. For example, the statement 'all dogs like meat' is a fact from which can be deduced a second statement 'Scamp is a dog therefore Scamp likes meat'. The second statement is a logical deduction from the first and you can make it with certainty.

Inference is someone's interpretation placed upon evidence and can, since it is based upon fact, also be highly reliable. However, since it is only an interpretation it may also contain elements of generalisation and assumption. As a result it might be nearer to speculation, which is a much more unreliable source of information. Thus with inference there cannot be absolute certainty and you must exercise judgment in evaluating it and take care in using it yourself.

Assumptions are not based on fact but are merely what we think could have happened. Their use arises when it is necessary to link to the facts some other information which seems to bear upon the problem but for which there is an absence of evidence.

Assumptions can be thought of as the building of a section of roadway to link up two other sections and without which you would come to a halt. When assumptions are used to carry an argument forward they are an acceptable addition since they help to build the reasoning path. If, however, they are used to reach a final decision there is need for caution. The result might be a decision without real foundation. In these instances, assumption should only be considered as a last result when other information is not available.

Although it is accepted that assumptions are not based on fact nevertheless they must still be plausible and realistic in the light of the circumstances described. It is essential that anyone reading an argument put forward should be able to follow the thought processes and so appreciate the reasons for the decision. In order to ensure this it is important when using assumptions to state clearly the evidence which has been considered in their formulation, the reasons for selecting and rejecting any particular points, and the precise form of the final assumptions made.

Assumptions can distort a case presentation and must be treated carefully. In particular, care should be taken to ensure that they are not used as a means of finding an easy solution to a difficult problem. Their use should always be kept to a minimum because in making them you move away from the original facts and this can result in a failure to recommend solutions to the real issues.

The extent to which other than absolutely unquestionable evidence is employed has always to be kept in mind, and in check, and it is wise to recognise that assumption is a danger area. **Hidden assumptions,** ie those accepted without real conscious awareness that they are assumptions, are the ones to guard against most. They may appear in a case, you might make them yourself or they may be made by someone in group discussion. The best advice is to develop a healthy scepticism and work on the premise that all assumptions should be challenged – particularly those 'everybody knows to be true'.

Despite the warnings, however, and provided the dangers are recognised, a combination of reasonable assumption and deduction are useful tools in working towards resolving difficult problems.

Skill development

Look over your work on Amfisbe Tools. Did you make any assumptions? Was it necessary to make them? Did you in fact recognise that they were assumptions? How far from the case facts did this take you?

Predict and evaluate

Predicting and evaluating consist firstly of predicting the outcomes of each alternative solution derived from studying the case, followed by their evaluation.

A straightforward way to start the task is to use the solutions as headings. Then under each heading list the outcome if that particular solution were adopted. You will probably expect to find that the outcome of technical solutions is easier to predict than ones that are concerned with the interaction of people. In recent years, however, behavioural scientists have found that human behaviour patterns are more predictable than had previously been supposed. Consequently, if you are aware of these patterns this helps in deciding how people might be expected to react in the case.

In predicting the outcomes of the alternative courses of action remember that:

a   Facts must be examined as they are, not as they should be, not as they are said to be, and certainly not as you would like them to be.
b   Preconceived ideas must be set firmly aside because they so often colour the interpretation of the facts.
c   All aspects of the problem should be approached with a challenging and sceptical attitude. Every detail must be examined logically with no answer accepted until it has been proved to be correct.
d   Hasty judgments should be avoided.
e   Close attention must be given to detail.
f   It is necessary to determine whether the problem is one to be corrected or one to be adjusted to as this will affect your decision making.

The advantages and disadvantages of each course of action can now be specified and considered prior to your final decision making.

Skill development

Make a point of observing people in normal working conditions and by so doing try to cultivate the ability to predict how they will act under certain circumstances. Any such sensitivity you are able to develop will prove to be most useful at this and other stages of handling a case. More than this it will be invaluable in real life situations.

Make decisions

In making your decisions you have to bear in mind your objectives since these will determine the type of action required. Will this need to be:

a   Interim action? This covers immediate measures to keep a system, a machine or the cooperation between people functioning.
b   Corrective action? This should lead to the elimination of the problem.
c   Adaptive action? If the problem cannot be eliminated then this type of action should be such that it results in the problem being minimised.

In advocating any action, it is important to state who is to be involved, what action that person should take and at what cost.

Although all aspects of problems have to be looked at separately in order to determine the causes, it is dangerous to continue to keep them separate because various facets may interact. To allow for this, after a solution has been decided upon check that it will not create difficulties because of its incompatibility with other key factors in the situation. A solution which is attractive on the surface is a poor one if, for example, it calls for more resources than are readily available.

A complication in reaching your decision can arise if a choice has to be made between long and short term goals which conflict. Bear in mind in connection with· this, and with making decisions in general, that in a business context the most desirable course is usually that which adopts the most profitable or the least costly of the alternatives.

Business problems are seldom simple to resolve. It is not that they are in themselves necessarily complex but one question often leads to another and the answers tend to raise more questions. Each of these questions has to be considered, individually decided upon and the solutions cross checked to ensure an overall consistency. It is this requirement for the making of many separate judgments from examining many facts which makes choice difficult. Ironically, in the end you might still be obliged to compromise between the ideal and what is actually feasible. Your aim can only be to make a final judgment which will result in what is best in the circumstances.

Cases parallel real life in that there are seldom clear cut answers, and no decision is likely to be completely risk free. Your answer may be good or bad but this largely depends upon the supporting argument and the use you make of the information available.

Once you have reached a decision as to the course of action to recommend, check it against the facts. Does it make sense? Does it solve the problem? Can it be successfully implemented?

Skill development

Now you can evaluate the ideas you thought of when practising the personalising of problems or your ideas for resolving the problems at Amfisbe (page 22). Do so by predicting the outcome of each course of action, then evaluate them and make your decision. What type of action would you recommend – interim, corrective or adaptive? After reading the following decide how you would implement your ideas.

Implement your strategy

The consideration you give to the implementation of your decision making is an important part of the study of a case since it is necessary to show that you have recognised what the constraints are and how they might be overcome or minimised. A brilliant solution to a problem is of no value if it cannot be successfully implemented.

Your consideration should cover such matters as:

a   *Responsibilities.* Will new responsibilities for the people concerned require there to be a major restructuring of the organisation? This must be the first question since the answer has a bearing on those that follow.

b   *Resources.* What constraints are there? When will machines, equipment and materials be available? Will competent staff be available? Will they need some training?

c   *Staff reaction.* A sensitivity to the human relations aspects can make or break any venture. Likely trouble areas must be sorted out before actual changes take place in order to ensure the active support of everyone concerned.

d   *Timing.* Decisions regarding this include thinking about whether or not a trial run of any method is desirable or practicable, and if all the proposals are to be implemented immediately.

e   *Alleviating disadvantages.* If your solution falls short of ideal then wherever possible draw up plans for coping with any disadvantages which cannot be overcome. Examples of this could be how to deal with any unavoidable redundancies, or arrangements for retraining if it were necessary to transfer staff.

Monitor progress

Since what happens in practice does not always follow what has been planned, suggestions for implementation should include some form of control procedure. This is to monitor progress, check that the plans laid down are progressing satisfactorily and allow for the taking of corrective or adaptive action necessary in the event of deviation from the plan.

You could build in a system on the following lines:

a   Devise a number of follow-up systems which check that instructions have been received, have been understood and are being carried out.

b   Incorporate a pattern of reporting procedures regarding progress of the recommended plan which can be checked against a previously drawn up time schedule.

c   Positively identify those responsible for carrying out the instructions so that all involved will be aware of who the key figures are. Make a point in your presentation of mentioning that it will be made clear to all concerned that authority has been delegated commensurate with the new responsibilities. If this is not so it can be a trouble area because it may mean that the person responsible for carrying out your plans has not got the authority required. Your mentioning this shows your awareness of one of the key factors in the successful implementation of the proposed plan.

d Set out a predetermined assessment schedule of progress dates.

e Provide some means of drawing attention as early as possible to any problems which might arise so that they can be dealt with quickly either by eliminating them or adapting the original plans.

Deal with change situations

Many cases incorporate a situation where there is to be a change in either a system, equipment, the environment or personnel. In fact, the case problems may have arisen as a result of this since conflict is very common at such a time. Your resolution of the problem itself might require changes to be made, and in writing about its implementation you should demonstrate an awareness of why change situations are potentially difficult and of how to handle them successfully.

Points to mention are that:

a People resist change not so much because of the change itself but because they will have to adjust to it. In particular, they fear a loss of status, earnings, job, skills, workmates and familiar surroundings. There is another, not always apparent, fear and that is of not being able to cope in the new situation. For obvious reasons, this is often covered up.

b These fears are very real to those concerned even when apparently unwarranted and irrational. Because of this, make the point in your presentation that management best serves the interests of all by consulting and communicating with employees. This should include: giving an explanation as to why the change is necessary; seeking employees' ideas – they often have good ones; and allaying fears.

c It is worth considering what it is that the case characters might like in the existing situation. If as much of this as possible is incorporated into the new arrangements, employees will be better satisfied and your explanations about this will further illustrate your understanding.

d There needs to be a willingness on the part of the people in the case to compromise and adopt a consultative rather than an autocratic approach. This again will demonstrate your awareness of the human relationship skills required in a difficult situation.

e Changes must be carefully monitored, and procedures should be set up to allow for this and to make adjustments as necessary.

f What may be seen as a minor change to management might appear as a major one to employees. It is often the failure to appreciate this that leads to conflict and it is something worth looking for in a case. Management does not always perceive the need for consultation, especially if the change appears to be a minor one. Employees read this as a lack of consideration and react in a manner which to them is quite reasonable in the circumstances. To management it frequently appears to be quite unreasonable, and so a course is set for trouble.

In considering any situation, it is always important to bear in mind that the reality of it is how the people concerned perceive it to be. Their perceptions can, and do, differ. The best you can do is to endeavour to see what all points of view are likely to be since this is a necessary precursor to reaching the optimum solution.

Skill development

In problem solving and decision making, case study skills and real life skill are indivisible. The development of either will benefit the other. Therefore, take what you have just read into your real life situation:

1 Are there any changes imminent?
2 Are these minor/major changes?
3 Have people been consulted/told about these?
4 Can you see ways of easing the changeover?

Application of skills

In this chapter, we have looked at problem solving and decision making and seen that this has consisted of:

a the setting of objectives.
b the creation and development of alternative approaches to resolving the problem.
c the prediction and evaluation of these alternative outcomes.
d decision making.
e the implementation and monitoring of the chosen approach.

We have also considered the usefulness and dangers of deduction, inference and assumption and the necessity for care and understanding in handling change situations.

Skill development

Armed with the techniques that you have learnt in this and the previous two chapters now work through the Meter Case which you will find at the beginning of Part 2 (page 77). You will find plenty of help in the comments but develop your own ideas before looking at these.

5 Writing a case analysis paper

Having dealt with the analysis and solving of the case problems we now move on to considering how to present the results of this work.

In the problem solving stages, cases may be discussed and analysed both individually and in groups. Similarly, the results can be presented individually or by a group. There is also a choice between written or oral form.

Whatever the method, do not underestimate the importance of the case presentation. Your work stands to lose or gain because the impact of your ideas will be affected by the quality of their communicating. If this is poor then no matter how searching your analysis and how brilliant your solution to the case problems your work will be undervalued. On the other hand, if your communicating is good it will enhance your work even if it is of only average quality. For this reason, skills in communication are as vital to the case study as those which have been dealt with in the previous chapters.

Written presentation

In presenting a written case analysis, it would be quite wrong to adopt the continuous prose essay style. The reasoning behind this becomes clear immediately if you relate the case situation to real life.

When a problem has to be investigated, it is usual for a subordinate to be delegated to do this and report his findings. One of the reasons for this is to save the time of his boss. Consequently, it would be expected that he should present his report such that the information is quickly apparent without every word being read. A means of achieving this is to write in brief paragraphs with subheadings and using lists and tables where possible. A similar style is acceptable for a case presentation.

Since studying cases aims to simulate real life, the format of a case analysis paper should also follow business conventions. If a report is required, for example, then this should be written in the same manner as a business report. If a letter is required, the then correct way to lay it out would be according to a standard business format with date, addresses, salutation and complimentary close included. Similarly with a memo, use the usual headings: To, From, Date, Reference and Subject. It is not sufficient just to write the message.

Skill development

If not already familiar with them, check on the recognised layout for a business letter, a memo, and a report, and keep a copy of these in your notes. A typewriting manual which you ought to be able to find in a library is a good source of reference for this.

Detail

Statements should be concise with repetition limited to where it is of specific advantage, for example, to emphasise a point. Flowery prose is inappropriate as is the covering up of a lack of knowledge with waffle. Take care, however, in regard to brevity particularly in written examinations:

a The wording must not be so brief as to be ambiguous or lacking in necessary information.
b The examiner can only mark the work you produce and is otherwise unaware of the depth of your knowledge.

Obviously you need to tread a careful path between brevity and verbosity, and the extent to which your reasoning is set down depends upon a number of factors:

a The amount of time available since this may necessitate a certain selectivity.
b The degree to which your analysis is based upon the facts given in the case as opposed to the use of your knowledge beyond this. The case facts have already been set out so they need only be mentioned briefly. If your conclusions are drawn solely from a combination of these facts then your writing can be confined to this. If, however, your argument relies heavily upon facts not in the case itself then these should be stated.
c The extent to which you are conventional. In general, the more unconventional your ideas the more detailed must be your explanation of them. Overseas students should note this particularly since in a paper for a British examining board they must be sure to explain clearly any aspect of their reasoning which they know to be specific to their own culture.

Adopting a role

The instructions that accompany a case frequently ask that a certain role be adopted. In some instances this may be that of the person who has to deal with the problem presented in the situation outlined. In others it might be a somewhat more detached role such as that of an outside consultant. It might be implied, as was seen in the Daynes Electronics case (page 9).

A general rule is that it is incorrect for the case to be dealt with as a theoretical exercise. In general also, the more successfully the role can be adopted and the more personally you can feel the problems the more realistic and practical will be the proposals you put forward.

Skill development

It is important to adopt the correct role from the outset when handling a case and vital to do so in an examination. Practise this by looking through the two cases in Part 2, Menlath Products (page 109) and Jamesons Limited (page 116). Jot down the appropriate role to adopt in each case.

Alternative forms

If a specific format such as a report is requested then this instruction must be followed. Failure to do so in an examination immediately incurs a loss of marks. If no guidance is given then the following format can usefully be followed since it progresses logically and in so doing mirrors the manner in which the case analysis should have been undertaken. Set out:

a   a concise presentation of the relevant data on the situation as given in the case; consider using a list for this.
b   a definition of the problem, including the factors causing it and their effects.
c   a statement of objectives, ie what you hope to achieve.
d   a statement and examination of the possible alternative courses of action, their implications, advantages and disadvantages.
e   your recommendations, including the criteria upon which they have been based.
f   your proposals for implementing the recommendations and monitoring the situation after they have been put into effect.

g additional comment such as any need you perceive for further research.

It is not essential that this format be followed exactly but any variation should present a similar logical progression through the analysis/problem solving process.

Answering questions

If you look at the case examples in Part 2 you will find that in many instances specific questions are asked. When questions are specified it is important that they be answered exactly as requested. It is a perpetual criticism by examiners that candidates fail to answer questions as asked and marks will be lost if instructions are not followed precisely.

When answering such questions a similar format to the one just suggested works well, provided that it is tailored to the question. Make sure that it is. The degree of emphasis, or indeed the need for some of the subheadings given, will of course vary but the advantage of bearing the format in mind is that it provides a logical framework and helps to reduce digression and waffle.

Skill development

Look at the questions set on two cases from Part 2. What exactly is required in each instance? Check against the key verbs list in the Appendix.

Summaries

There is a good argument for preparing a summary, since this is often a real life requirement. This is because the purpose of a summary is to state briefly but clearly the recommendations and the most important reasons for these having been reached. This is obviously useful to the busy reader.

A summary often appears as the first item so that a quick impression of the whole work can be gained. It is in fact more effective if actually written last but still appears as the first item. The total information obtained and thought given can then be drawn upon to produce a statement which should as a result be all the more convincing.

Reports

This is a common form of case presentation since it offers a businesslike framework for writing up the analysis findings and recommendations. If you write a report then it must be written as though it were the result of a real life investigation. It must give information, report findings and put forward ideas and recommendations. Also as in real life, it must be accurate, clear and brief.

Since a case report is likely to be recommending a course of action, the arguments for this action must be developed skilfully, logically and persuasively. The facts, your interpretation, and the problem solving ideas you have developed should be written down and then sifted to reject any which do not support your recommendations.

Order of presentation

First, choose headings for the main divisions and then list subheadings as necessary. Use a consistent system of numbering if this clarifies the presentation or if the numbers could be needed for reference.

A logical order of presentation for a report is:

- Introduction
- Body of the report
- Conclusions and recommendations

Introduction

The introduction is best written after the main body of the report has been drafted since you use it to give a broad general view of the material. Make it as interesting as possible by singling out significant points but take care not to distort facts by undue emphasis.

Adopt the following subdivisions as appropriate:

a   the name and job title of the person for whom the report is intended.
b   the purpose and terms of reference (the reason why such a report has been deemed necessary)
c   background information needed to ensure the reader's understanding, such as the sequence of past events leading to the present problem.
d   a note indicating the arrangement of the main sections so that the reader is aware of how the subject matter is to be developed.
e   a brief summary, if desired, of the results, conclusions and/or recommendations.

Body of the report

The body of the report covers the main presentation of information and should be arranged in an easy to follow logical sequence. One of the most effective ways of ensuring this is to present each main piece of information as a separate section.

Conclusions and recommendations

Conclusions and recommendations summarise the discussion in the body of the report and must not therefore contain any new ideas. Your statements need to be emphatic, unqualified, clear and consistent with the introduction.
This is the place to:

a Restate the findings.
b State the recommendations based on the findings.
c State what action should be taken as a result of the recommendations, and by whom.
d Emphasise the significance of the subject matter.

Throughout, bear in mind the real life purpose of a report. In effect, this should place the recipient in a position to take necessary action, knowing that it will be based on thoroughly investigated circumstances. The report should put him in the picture as thoroughly as if he had carried out the investigation himself. Similarly, a case report reader should feel as familiar with the case as if he had analysed it personally.

Style

Whatever the format of your presentation, adopt a businesslike tone and write in a simple functional style. Avoid writing in a vague or abstract manner, eg: 'the current tendency of unemployment levels'. This would be better written as the firm statement 'employment is now rising by 15 per cent each year'. Write in short sentences because this reduces the need for explanations or interpolations in brackets. Punctuate sparingly.
Aim to write quickly when drafting since this aids the flow of words. It does, however, increase any tendency to verbosity and pruning may be necessary later.
At the revision stage, objective self criticism is needed to ensure that all unnecessary words, sentences and paragraphs are deleted. In addition, grammar and spelling have to be corrected and phraseology polished. You might find it necessary to rephrase sections and make deletions or

additions in order to expand or clarify the text, change the emphasis and rectify errors.

Ensure that you only include ideas which help to explain what is recommended, and why. Omit facts found to be irrelevant to your decision making, however reluctant you might be to leave out information you have put a lot of time into obtaining. While it is not necessary to specify all the possibilities which might have been developed, mention any definitely supportable alternatives which have been considered and rejected. This is often an effective means of justifying your choice.

The most obvious defects to guard against in regard to subject matter include the omission of points essential to an understanding of the analysis, the inclusion of irrelevant or tedious detail and the placing of information in the wrong section.

Final check

Before submitting the presentation ask yourself:

1 Has everything necessary been included, anything unnecessary been excluded?
2 Is the development appropriate and logical so that every idea, fully explained, leads naturally to the ideas that follow?
3 Are all the statements correct?
4 Is the balance right or has too much emphasis been placed on some relatively insignificant point because it deals with a matter of personal interest?
5 Are paragraphs of a reasonable length with clear and well structured sentences?
6 Have technical terms been explained?
7 Has everything necessary for the readers' understanding been included?
8 Do the illustrations convey their messages clearly? Are they captioned precisely and informatively? Do the references in the text tally?
9 Is the work attractively presented with a consistent format, lettering or numbering as required, a good layout and clear references?

Finally, consider if the aim has been achieved, ie the production of a clear and concise piece of work with the main points arranged in the most suitable sequence and presented in such a manner that they stand out effectively?

Most people who mark case presentations would agree that it is almost impossible to completely eliminate the subjective element. Capitalise on this. A neat, well presented paper makes a good impression on a weary marker!

Present the work in a folder neatly labelled. Take the trouble to set out a title page and a contents page. Include a few blank pages at the end which the marker can use for comments.

Conveying information is an important aspect of most people's work and the written presentation of a case provides an opportunity for you to practise and improve your effectiveness in this. Make the most of it.

Skill development

As shown, an important aspect of case study work lies in communicating your proposed solutions to the case problems. A written presentation is a common means of doing so. Such a presentation should follow real life conventions with regard to layout and be written in a real life business style. Practise this by working through the case in Part 2 titled 'A question of training' (page 85) and write the report asked for. You will find full notes against which to check your ideas.

6 Oral presentation

Although case study examinations require a written analysis, the very nature of the course work involves a considerable use of oral skills. Not only do ideas need to be put across persuasively and tactfully in small group discussion but you are likely to be called upon to present either part or the whole of a case analysis to your full study group.

On your own

This analysis might be the result of work by a syndicate for which you have been elected spokesperson, or it might be the result of individual study. Whichever it is, remember that the manner in which ideas are expressed greatly influences their acceptance. In presenting them, your task is to gain this acceptance and you must therefore aim for a first class delivery.

One of the main differences between the oral and the written presentation lies in the character and environment of the audience. Written presentations are usually assessed under controlled conditions by someone informed in the subject and interested in you – your tutor. Your audience may not be so informed and the onus is on you to arouse and retain interest. To do this you must ensure that the presentation is organised in such a way that the audience is constantly aware of the sequence and direction of your comments.

On any occasion when you are required to present a detailed statement of your analysis orally then think of this as giving a talk to an audience and prepare for it meticulously. Not only will your words and therefore your ideas be more likely to gain acceptance by the audience but your knowledge of being well prepared will give you confidence when the time comes to begin.

Do not be tempted to carry your preparation to the extreme by writing out your analysis word for word and then reading it. This will not sound natural because you do not write as you speak. The written word is generally more carefully chosen and the sentence structure more complex. As a result, when this is read aloud it appears artificial and lacking in what are important aspects of the spoken word – spontaneity and sincerity.

Reading also removes the possibility of eye contact, of the sweeping glance which allows each person to feel personally addressed.

A useful method of preparation is to prepare an outline so that your main thoughts and comments are on the paper but not the actual words. If you use this as your guide in speaking you will have a good prop yet still be able to respond to audience reaction because you will be speaking to and not at them. Grammatically the result may not be perfect and there may be unnecessary repetition but the overall effect will be better.

In order to overcome initial nerves you might compromise by writing out the introduction in detail or memorise it. You might also consider writing out the recommendations to ensure that nothing is omitted.

Some people find it useful to make notes on cards. If you do this make sure that the writing is large enough to read from waist level. These notes may only be key words but they help to keep your discourse flowing along a previously determined path and give confidence. Holding the cards also gives you something to do with your hands.

Take positive steps to avoid the public speaker's nightmare of dropping all the cards. Punch a hole in the top left hand corner and thread a treasury tag through or make a string loop.

With the group

All the points mentioned in connection with individual delivery and those to follow under other headings apply equally to a group presentation. There are, however, several important differences in this situation:

a   You have an obligation to the group to make a positive contribution.
b   You might be constrained in your comments by having been asked to deal with just a specific area – and it might not be one that you know much about.
c   You have the support of the group.
d   You do not have sole control of the presentation and might have to be satisfied with an assessment from your tutor or a reception by an audience less good than if you had done it on your own.

Your group will judge your contribution according to the measure of their success and you will undoubtedly feel their pleasure or lack of it, whether this is verbalised or not.

Assessment criteria

The assessment of an oral presentation whether it be a formal statement or informal comment is likely to take into account the following:

a the quality and thoroughness of your analysis.
b the practicability of your recommendations.
c the quality of any visual aids you use.
d the organisation of your presentation.
e your delivery and poise.
f your dress and posture.
g your movements and mannerisms.
h your ability to answer questions and defend the position taken.

Success with *a* and *b* is likely to arise from a careful application of the suggestions contained in previous chapters. Visual aids *c* are the topic of the next chapter. Let us now attend to the remaining points, that is *d–h*.

Organisation of presentation

This is more difficult in the group situation. Work responsibilities have to be divided and group consensus is needed for decisions regarding such matters as the roles to be adopted and the order and mode of presentation. Discussing these subtracts from the much needed time available for case work but you will be more than compensated in terms of the experience of group interaction which you gain.

It might be decided that the group presentation should take the form of role play with each person adopting the role of a character mentioned in the narrative of the case or of one who could be associated with it. In general, but in this instance in particular, it may be felt that a rehearsal is needed. Most group presentations do benefit from one. This consists of a talking through within the group of what each person is to do and has the advantage of making sure that everything is covered. It helps to give confidence because everyone knows what to do.

Whether it be a group or an individual presentation, the content should follow a logical progression and in many instances this will be as that suggested for case analysis in the previous chapters.

It is worthwhile paying special attention to the beginning and to the end. A good opening is important in arousing interest and in gaining the attention of the audience. In a case study presentation a useful ploy is to start by relating the subject matter to some topical issue or to some matter of specific concern to the audience. Equally important is a good finish, something punchy or amusing, because this will leave the audience with a good impression.

Delivery and poise

Start positively to ensure that attention is gained immediately. Establishing contact as suggested above helps. Vary your speed of delivery and bear in mind that nervousness tends to increase speed. In general also, the larger the audience the more slowly you should speak.

Your speech must be clear with the volume varied but of course always loud enough to be heard by everyone. Aim for a medium pitch but do not cultivate an unvarying one as this becomes most monotonous if listened to for long.

If you can vary the mood by injecting a little humour then so much the better. This will depend upon its appropriateness to the case situation. Emphasise main points by rephrasing and repeating them. Use pauses for effect, to emphasise a point and to give the audience time to take in some important comment made.

Taking a good deep breath before starting is an often quoted tip for helping to steady the nerves. It helps but take care. Too much breath makes the words rush out and might make you appear even more nervous. Conversely, too little breath causes the voice to fade away. Controlled breathing must be your aim.

Be natural in your speech and manner and above all be enthusiastic. If you appear bored with the whole thing your audience certainly will be!

Dress and posture

You will most certainly be looked at so choose clothes that will not distract the audience from what you are saying. What you wear should be normal for that occasion and something in which you can feel comfortable and therefore forget about. This point about comfort applies particularly to shoes.

Clothes can affect your posture in that they may influence the way you stand. Try to adopt a relaxed stance. Do not lean against anything that could move easily – the audience will be more concerned with wondering whether or not it is going to topple over than in listening to you!

Keep your head up, otherwise your words will be lost. Look at the audience – you should receive valuable feedback as to whether what you are saying is being heard and understood. Beware of fixing your gaze on any one point, the audience might wonder what they are missing and start casting gazes in that direction.

Movement and mannerisms

Your movements should not include useless, fidgety gestures because these are distracting. Any movement you make should be with the specific intention of supporting what you say. Examples of this are stepping forward – this indicates that an important point is coming which the audience should not miss; pushing the hand down and to one side which indicates rejection or disapproval; and the well known political speaker's use of the pointed finger.

Do make a concentrated effort to eliminate any known mannerisms such as jangling money in the pocket, fiddling with jewellery or pacing up and down like a caged lion. Get a friend to check if you have any distracting mannerisms without being aware of it.

Answering questions

You must be able to defend your recommendations when questions are asked. In preparing for this, try to visualise the sort of questions which might be asked. You can then set about mentally answering them. If you prepare well and have a detailed knowledge of the case and related information you will be more capable of answering any questions which might arise.

Do not hurry into an answer. Buy time if needed by asking 'Has the question been understood?', 'Have I got the question clear?'

If a question is not very audible or was awkwardly put repeat it or rephrase it. Never treat a question with contempt even if you think that it is not very important. No doubt it will be to the questioner and it is usually possible to find some comment to make.

Skill development

Consider the cases you have already worked on. If you were presenting your solutions orally what questions do you think the audience might ask?

Manner towards audience

Aim to give an impression that you are addressing each person individually by using the device of eye contact referred to earlier. Be careful though. Let it be a sweeping glance. Do not fix your gaze solidly upon one person otherwise he will wonder what is wrong and start fidgeting.

Treat your audience courteously; they are being courteous in listening to you. Forget yourself. Concentrate on them and on making what you have to say worth listening to. Consciously try to make opportunities to speak in public or speak out in a group discussion or meeting. This is especially important if you have been previously inclined to avoid doing so. You might find yourself gaining in all kinds of ways!

7 Illustrating case presentations

More is retained of what is read and of what is said if it is accompanied by some form of illustration. Indeed, considerable detail may be recalled if it can be associated with a picture and you should use this to advantage by supporting your presentation with charts, diagrams and other visual aids.

Primary considerations

If a visual aid is to be of value it must be remembered. The primary aim in designing it is to ensure that the most significant information is immediately obvious. Anything that is confused is worse than nothing because it will create further confusion.

Omit anything irrelevant. To this end it is essential to decide at the outset your purpose in using a graphic form to support your presentation. If what you produce does not really convey the message better than words then seriously question whether it should be used at all.

The fact that an illustration looks good is not sufficient justification for its inclusion, although an exception might be something which has been inserted solely to draw the eye in order to focus attention upon the main object. This is much exploited in advertising; for example, a pretty girl perched on the bonnet of a car. Do take care if you adopt this ploy not to divert attention from your main illustration. The same warning applies to anything funny. The use of humour is excellent and does aid the memory but make sure that it is your message that is remembered and not just the humour.

Reinforcing written work

An example of an ideal occasion for illustrating your information, and incidentally a means of cutting down on reading time, is when a large number of complicated statistics have to be included. The following is a simple example but still conveys little at first glance:

'Sales for the Fresh–2–U Dairy Company in 1980 totalled £380 000 made up as follows: butter £76 000, dairy cream £95 000, eggs £66 500, ice cream £95 000 and orange juice £47 500. In 1982 the total was £530 000 made up as follows: butter £66 250, dairy cream £132 500, eggs £103 750, ice cream £95 000 and orange juice £132 500.'

When arranged in the form of a table (Fig 1) the information is immediately clearer.

	1980 (£000s)	1982 (£000s)
Butter	76.00	66.25
Dairy cream	95.00	132.50
Eggs	66.50	103.75
Ice cream	95.00	95.00
Orange juice	47.50	132.50
Total sales	380.00	530.00

Fig 1 Fresh-2-U Dairy Company – comparison of sales 1980/82

If you then proceed a step further and produce a chart the information is even more readily seen. Before doing so, however, you must decide what kind of chart to use and this depends upon the interpretation you wish to make of the data and the point you want to prove. In other words, what picture do you want your readers to retain.

As a simple example of the different interpretations possible – Fig 1 table read vertically shows sales in categories and the total for the year; read horizontally it shows how sales in each of the categories differed in the two years given. Further if the table is extended over a number of years (Fig 2), trends can be discerned from a horizontal reading.

	1979 (£000s)	1980 (£000s)	1981 (£000s)	1982 (£000s)	1983 (£000s)
Butter	82.00	76.00	70.00	66.25	66.00
Dairy cream	95.00	95.00	107.50	132.50	110.00
Eggs	68.00	66.50	85.00	103.75	97.50
Ice cream	108.00	95.00	109.00	95.00	115.00
Orange juice	41.00	47.50	77.00	132.50	140.00
Total sales	394.00	380.00	448.50	530.00	528.50

Fig 2 Fresh-2-U Dairy Company – comparison of sales over the period 1979–83

By portraying your information in the form of a chart you are making comparisons. The comparisons you make depend upon what you want to prove and this therefore depends upon your narrative. Only when you have this settled can you begin to determine the type of chart to use.

Let us look at some of the alternative ways of presenting the facts about the Fresh–2–U Dairy Company:

a If the point to illustrate is the relative size of the sales of each item as a proportion of the total, an obvious choice is a pie chart (Fig 3) as this gives a clear impression of being a complete whole. The relative size of the segments is also easy to judge at a glance. In designing these charts the number of items has to be considered since it is generally best to restrict pie chart segments to four or five. Another deciding factor is the complexity of the data. From a practical viewpoint pie charts can only be used where the figures are simple because otherwise they are difficult to construct.

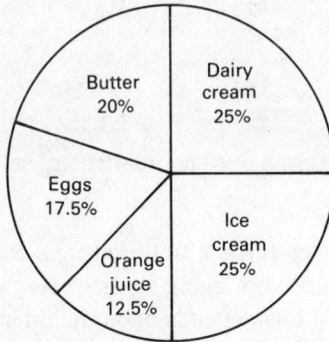

Fig 3   Fresh-2-U Dairy Company – 1980 sales pie chart

An alternative to the pie chart, and usually a better choice where several totals have to be portrayed, is the percentage bar chart (Fig 4). The entire bar represents 100 per cent, ie in this case the entire sales.

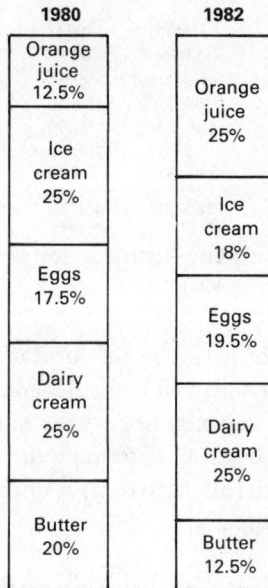

Fig 4   Percentage bar chart

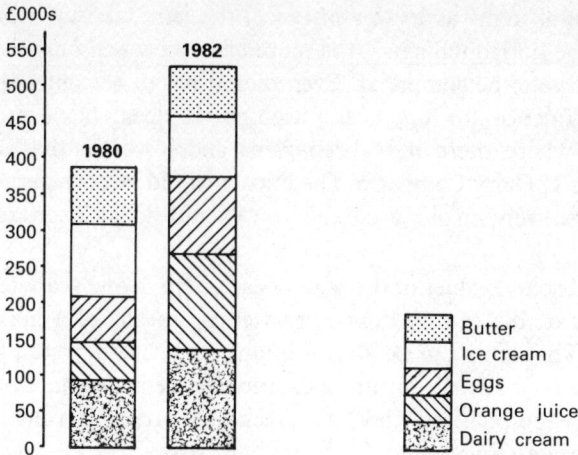

Fig 5   Absolute value bar chart

The boxes could be shaded, with a key to identify the items (Fig 5).

b   If the comparison to be brought out is the change in the sales values of each of the items in the years 1980 and 1982, this can be achieved by a variation of the bar chart to show the absolute values (Fig 5). In this instance it is best to put the most important item at the bottom of the column since it is only this which can be compared really accurately at first sight. This type of chart has the advantage of being compact but may require an extended vertical axis or a small scale.

An alternative form of bar chart to achieve the same purpose is that shown in Fig 6. A disadvantage of this is fairly obvious. When there

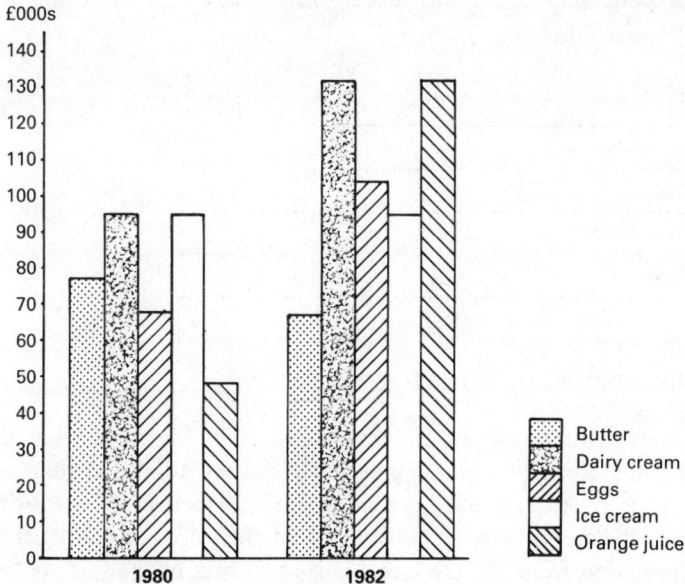

Fig 6   Vertical bar chart

are several items as in this instance, the bars take up a lot of space along the horizontal axis. It is more effective when only two or three items have to be compared. Even then it has to be confined to a short time sequence for practical purposes. It does, however, illustrate clearly where there have been gains and losses in the sales of the Fresh-2-U Dairy Company. The impact would be considerably greater of course were colour used and you should do so in producing your charts.

c If the absolute values of the sales of each item in one year only are to be compared this can be done very well by means of a horizontal bar chart. The items can be shown in any sequence depending upon the point to be made. If, for instance, the relative importance of each item is to be emphasised then a descending order of value would be appropriate (Fig 7).

1982 Sales (£000s)

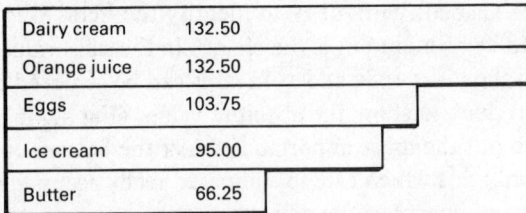

Dairy cream	132.50
Orange juice	132.50
Eggs	103.75
Ice cream	95.00
Butter	66.25

Fig 7 Horizontal bar chart, including values

If the uneven contribution of each item is the message to be conveyed then the items need to be placed in an order which emphasises this (Fig 8).

1982 Sales

| Ice cream |
| Butter |
| Dairy cream |
| Eggs |
| Orange juice |

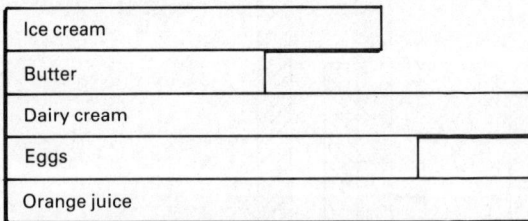

Fig 8 Horizontal bar chart, excluding values

d Trends and fluctuations are best portrayed by means of a line graph. Instead of using blocks to represent the figures, as in a bar chart, only a dot is used. A trend over a period of time can then easily be shown on a small chart. Fig 9 is an illustration of this form of chart using the information from the table in Fig 2 in respect of the sales of butter, orange juice and ice cream.

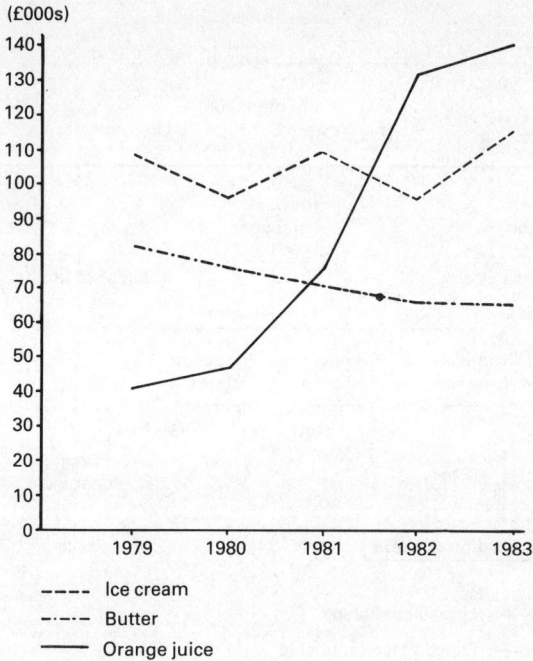

(£000s)

- - - - Ice cream
- ·- ·- Butter
――― Orange juice

Fig 9   Sales of butter, ice cream and orange juice 1979–83 line graph

It would be best to use a line graph if you have used in your narrative sentences such as:

a   'Sales of ice cream fell back in 1980 and 1982 but rose in 1981 and 1983.'
b   'Sales of butter showed a steady decline in the period under review.'
c   'Sales of orange juice have increased sharply over the past five years.'

There are many variations on the theme of charts. The few illustrated here are intended to demonstrate how clearly in your own mind you need to keep the picture you intend to convey to your readers.

The most common form of chart found in case studies is the organisation chart and Fig 10 shows the organisation chart which might be drawn in response to the first question on The Western Sausage Co Ltd case which can be found in Part 2, page 99. Although there are alternative forms which convey more appropriately the way in which an organisation is set up, the family tree type of chart remains the most common. The pattern of these usually flows downwards from the most senior post through the posts with less and less authority to those with the least of all.

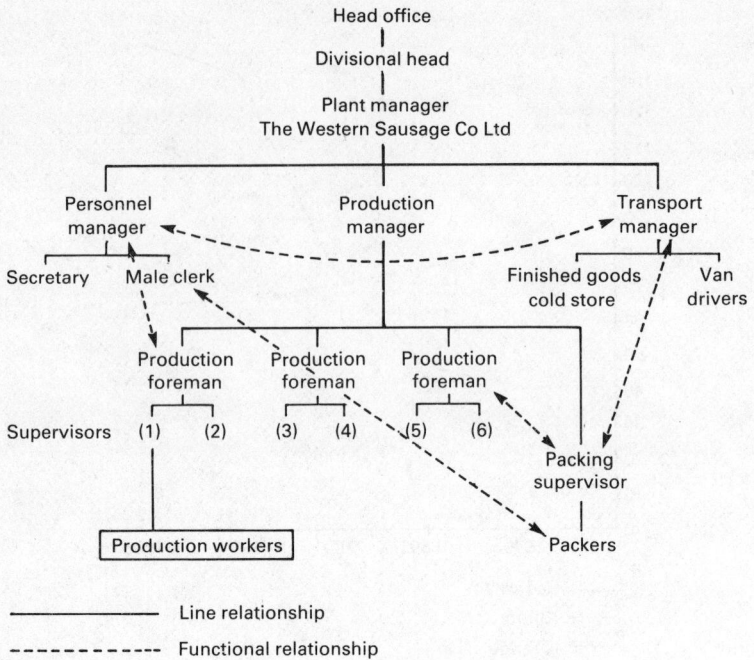

```
                        Head office
                             |
                        Divisional head
                             |
                        Plant manager
                    The Western Sausage Co Ltd
         ┌───────────────────┼───────────────────┐
   Personnel              Production            Transport
    manager ◄──────        manager       ──────► manager
      └─┐        ─ ─ ─ ─ ─ ─ ─ ─ ─ ─ ─ ─ ─ ─ ┌─┘
Secretary   Male clerk            Finished goods   Van
                                   cold store     drivers
              ┌──────┬──────────┬──────────┐
         Production  Production  Production
          foreman    foreman     foreman
          ┌──┴──┐    ┌──┴──┐    ┌──┴──┐
Supervisors (1)  (2)  (3)  (4)  (5)  (6)
                                          Packing
                                          supervisor
                                             |
     ┌────────────────────────┐          Packers
     │  Production workers     │
     └────────────────────────┘
```

—————————— Line relationship

- - - - - - - - - - Functional relationship

Fig 10   The Western Sausage Co Ltd organisation chart

The advantage is that they are easily understood and this is perhaps the major argument for their popularity.

Choose for impact

Simple graphics are usually the most effective form of visual communication and selecting the significant points and confining yourself to them is one of the skills needed.

A careful consideration of what is best written and what is best illustrated is also important because too many illustrations interrupt the flow of the narrative and become a distraction. A means of avoiding this is to present them as an appendix. They can appear in the same order as they would if part of the text, are given appropriate titles, and are numbered, Appendix 1, Appendix 2 and so on. This number is the reference to be used in the text and if any do not need to be so referenced then very likely they are unnecessary and should be rejected.

Supporting oral presentation

When you make an oral presentation, listening is the means by which information reaches the audience. It varies considerably but nevertheless the amount of time anyone can listen attentively is limited, even if the subject is of personal interest. You will make a greater impact, keep attention longer and leave a more lasting impression if you add sight to sound. Using an overhead projector, showing a film or slides, drawing a diagram on the board or putting up a previously prepared one are some of the ways of doing this. They also ensure that everyone present has the same mental picture and increase understanding of the subject matter.

As the presenter you will find such visuals useful as an *aide-memoire*. They help you to keep to the predetermined order of your presentation, and the structure and direction of this is also more apparent to your audience. You can use visual aids to emphasise key points, thus enabling you to cut down on the amount of oral description and save time.

In order to achieve all this, it is essential for a visual aid to be well prepared. Make it simple, bold and eye catching. Do not, however, be too ingenious or else people will be more interested in the mechanics of the aid than in the information you intend it to convey. Also avoid excessive detail or the audience will devote so much attention to sorting this out that what you say will be lost. Neither must you show all the information at once, since the audience will read this quickly and not wish to listen to you repeating it. A means of avoiding this is to prepare a series of charts or one chart upon which you can place additions. If you are using an overhead projector you can prepare a basic transparency plus overlays or cover the portion of the transparency not being dealt with using a sheet of paper.

Your presentation of the aid is important in a number of ways. Make sure that everyone can see it from where they are sitting and take care that you do not block their view. Do not talk to the board or screen upon which the illustration appears – you still need to look at the people. Using a pointer rather than your finger will allow you to stand more easily to the side and at least three-quarters on to your listeners.

Because a visual aid attracts, that is where the attention of the audience will be so long as it is on view. Remove it when finished with. Do not, however, take it away so quickly that people have not had time to digest it fully otherwise they will feel cheated and spend the next few minutes wondering what they have missed or asking their neighbours. Remember also to pause when first presenting the aid so that the audience does not have to try to understand it as well as you at the same time.

Disadvantages of visual aids

The disadvantages of visual aids that are common to both written and oral presentations are cost and the very considerable amount of time required to produce a good aid. The greatest disadvantages concern oral presentations. Things go wrong. In order to avert disaster and not appear inefficient you must always be prepared to carry on unperturbed without the aid. It must be an aid to you, not a control upon you. This also applies in another sense. Decide upon your presentation structure based upon your information. Do not base your structure upon your visual aids. To do so will not only prove to be absolutely disastrous should anything go wrong but could well place you in a straitjacket and not allow you to be flexible and responsive to your audience.

Use or not?

It is your decision whether or not to include visual aids, but the criterion upon which to base this is clear. An illustration should only be used when there is a clear need or objective for it.

When you have established this, its use should be planned so that it is an integral part of the presentation and not just something added to look good. Then without a doubt, the additional effectiveness of your presentation will more than repay the extra time spent on it.

8 Case study examinations

A major aim in studying cases is to develop the ability to make decisions about action. Consequently, case study examinations seek to test this ability.

They fall broadly into two categories; those where the case is unseen, and those where the case is distributed prior to the examination. In the latter instance you can seek help, but in an unseen case examination you have to rely solely upon the techniques you have learnt and the expertise you have acquired previously from dealing with cases.

Practice makes perfect

The necessity for practice in working with cases cannot be emphasised too strongly. In particular, no one should consider entering for a case study examination without such practice.

When confronted with a case presenting several aspects of a problem, especially in a time-constrained examination, your problem solving and decision making techniques need to be consciously, but effortlessly, applied. If you have become familiar with handling cases, you ought to be efficient in ascertaining and organising the facts. As a result, it should be possible to do the work effectively, with confidence, and accommodate the time limitations.

However great your working experience, learning and practising case study skills is still necessary. An experienced real life problem solver is not automatically good at dealing with a written case. He might normally be able to resolve problems adequately, even with flair, but may not have developed the analytical, data searching skills necessary for handling written cases. Another skill he could lack is that of presenting his analysis and resultant decision making in a manner acceptable to a case study examiner.

Studying alone

If you are preparing for an examination without any form of tuition, the comments elsewhere regarding groups and courses will not normally apply. You can, however, usefully adapt some of the methods mentioned.

Try reading and thinking about a case over a period of days before writing it up. Alternatively, and this you definitely need to do prior to an unseen case study examination, take up an unfamiliar case and allocate the stated length of time allowed in the examination to dealing with it. Do not feel this to be a waste of time when there is no one to read and assess your work. If you put it away and look at it again after a few days, you ought then to be able to form some sort of assessment of it yourself. Avoid doing so immediately you finish. At that time you are likely to think it either absolutely brilliant or be utterly depressed by the results of your efforts!

Through practice of this kind you will certainly find out how easy or difficult the task is for you. This should determine how much practice you need to undertake and will alert you to how effectively you can contain your writing within the time allowed.

Is it possible to overcome the disadvantages of studying alone? Can you persuade any of your friends or colleagues to discuss some cases with you? If you belong to a professional association, is it possible through this to get in touch with other students in a similar position? If so, you could send each other your written case work for comment, and possibly meet occasionally for discussion. A word of warning, you need to be absolutely honest with one another. Constructive criticism is what is needed but unfortunately in such situations it is easier to give way to mutual admiration. It is after all very pleasant to receive praise and give it but by itself this will not be of real benefit to either of you.

Preparing for the examination

In examinations where the case is given out in advance, there is obviously the motivation and the opportunity to study and discuss it and to try to spot the questions.

Studying the case is necessary, discussing it useful, spotting questions a possible danger. Do not confine your work to areas spotted as being ripe for questioning upon – you might not do so accurately.

You can nevertheless approach your preparation for the examination by reasonably assessing the odds. These can often be reduced considerably by studying past examination papers to see if there are areas which crop up regularly. Such papers are usually available from the examining board for a few pence.

A more reliable aid, and one which instead of narrowing your preparation sharpens and focuses it, is to analyse the type of questions asked. Do they call for the setting down of a lot of theory or do they require the utilising of individual experience? Do they usually ask for charts and tables? Are the questions fairly general or very specific? Is the candidate required to give a lot of detail, quote research, name names?

It is safer to get the feel of past papers and a general understanding of their style in this way rather than prepare specific answers to anticipated specific questions. If you do the latter there is the danger of using a prepared answer for one question to answer another which is only similar. By so doing you will not answer it specifically and this is one of the criticisms constantly levelled at candidates by examiners. Do not lose marks for this reason, it is so unnecessary.

If the case is given out in advance, you can work through all the stages of analysis described in earlier chapters. In your preparation make the analysis as broad as possible with a good number of alternatives. It will then be easier to tailor answers to the questions as asked. Aim for complete familiarity with the case and well organised notes. If these can be taken into the examination room, the various points can then be rapidly assembled as the basis for your answers. If you are not allowed to take notes in, then the very fact of having organised them should mean that your mind is similarly well organised.

As a word of hope, remember that cases do not generally have right or wrong answers. The quality of a solution depends to a large extent upon the supporting arguments and use made of the information available. If you have practised, you should have sharpened these skills.

What are examiners looking for?

At first sight this might seem to be a difficult question to answer. In general, examinations test ability and knowledge. In particular, case study examinations test an ability to apply knowledge and to add that personal ingredient of experience.

As mentioned previously, since everyone's experience is unique a case analysis produced by one person may differ significantly from that produced by someone else. The question then is – how can the examiner judge such a variety of scripts? He will do so by looking for:

a   an organised presentation of data.
b   a positive identification of the problems with a clear distinction made between these and the symptoms, and an ability to distinguish between fact and opinion.
c   flair and originality in establishing alternatives, skill in presenting negative and positive aspects, and evidence of the extent to which all possibilities have been explored.
d   a rational, skilled evaluation of the alternatives, and a well reasoned substantiation of recommendations which closely relate to the problems.
e   precision of strategy and completeness of plans for implementation, together with an understanding of the need for control and monitoring.
f   good appearance, correct grammar, clarity of expression and legibility.

Hints for success

Examination success is not a question of good luck, although there is often an element of this. It is strategy and planning which turns knowledge and ability into success.

The following list of points to remember apply to all examinations:

a Obey precisely the instructions given on the paper.

b Study each question carefully, analyse it and give the kind of answer required.

c Answer the questions as set in the paper, not as you would like them to be set. Do not write down everything you know about the subject; just write about the aspects asked for.

d Make notes and assemble them into a coherent whole before beginning to write.

e Take care with presentation. Although usually carrying only a small percentage of the marks, the overall appearance of the script matters a great deal because of the image it projects. A neat presentation cannot fail to make a good impression on a weary examiner who so often has to struggle through masses of rambling and badly written examination scripts.

f Unless advised otherwise, hand in your working notes with a line drawn through to show that they are not part of your answer. They will not normally be referred to, but in some instances if an answer is marginal there is provision for reading working notes in order to find possible reasons for giving extra marks.

The following series of points refer to case study examinations in particular:

a Relate to theory – once the case is firmly established in your mind, mentally review the material covered in your course for points which might be relevant. Apply your knowledge. Test ideas against recognised theories and use them in presenting your recommendations.

b Demonstrate the relevance of your solution to current trends. Higher marks are likely to be awarded for work related to what is happening in the real world, where this is applicable. It shows awareness, wider reading and an ability to apply knowledge.

c Use opinions and ideas wisely. Personal opinion is acceptable, even if it differs from the norm, always provided a sensible and reasonable case is made for it and bias is avoided. There is always room for the innovator if his ideas are well supported by reasoned argument and comment.

d Apply an analytical, critical, questioning approach. This is, of course, a skill which can be developed through practice. Make use of your tutor if you have one. Make use of books of cases which are available; some have suggested outline answers, but develop your own ideas. Obtain as much feedback as you can from others by participating in group discussions. It is sometimes agonising to offer one's brainchild for dissection; but defending it, maybe even letting it die, is necessary for good preparation. You need to be aware of possible flaws in your reasoning processes in order to avoid them in future.

e Illustrate – use charts and diagrams where possible. Apart from clarifying issues they make for variety. But make them work for you; do not use them just for decoration.

f Follow the earlier suggestions with regard to reading through and connecting with a case. Remember that this has to be immediate in an unseen case examination so must be well practised. A previously cultivated rigorous questioning approach helps because efficiency in gathering and organising factual information increases as a result of practice.

g Follow a structure of analysis and decision making such as that suggested. Not only will this encourage a logical progression of thought, but the familiarity of it will give you confidence.

Planning your time

Failure to plan one's time is the cause of many examination failures, therefore:

a Prepare a timetable. Allocate time to answering the questions in proportion to the marks they carry.

b Stick to the timetable. It is easy to be carried away by issues about which you know a great deal or which are of particular interest. Minor matters should be given minor attention. Stick to major matters and do not get side-tracked.

c If you run short of time on a question, jot down in note form the rest of the points you were going to make. It is worth remembering that the first few marks on a question are usually easy to get, the last few very difficult.

d Make sure that all your time is used fruitfully. Do not spend a lot of time working out detail which you may not use. Practice will help you to develop a knack of knowing what is important.

e Allow time for revision of your work and reading through in order to ensure that it 'hangs together' and that there are no obvious errors.

Pitfalls to avoid

a *Panic.* As suggested under 'Hints for success', follow a structure. If you work through this, it helps to overcome feelings of panic because it encourages positive thought and should start the ideas flowing.

b *Re-telling the case.* The examiner is already familiar with it!

c *Failing to identify relevant and important points.* Underline key facts, note points of theory. Read and re-read the case until you 'feel' it. The more it becomes real the less the danger of missing important issues.

d *Overstressing numbers.* This is easily done; numbers often command undue attention perhaps because they appear concrete and something you can get your teeth into. Manipulating them may be important for the analysis but do avoid taking a mass of figures, analysing them and then ending up with another mass equally hard to understand!

9 Do not expect it to be easy

Although studying cases is an interesting way of learning, no doubt there will be occasions when you find it hard, bewildering and tough on the ego. It is especially tough if you are experienced in handling problems in your familiar work surroundings because you may not find them so easy to deal with in the unfamiliar case settings. This is quite usual and the reasons are not hard to find. Work knowledge grows over a period of time and becomes familiar. You are comfortable with it, know what to expect and are experienced in handling whatever crops up. There are likely to be accepted precedents for decision making and you have built up your competence as a result of trial and error and proven success.

Lack of training

In common with most people, however, you may not have been taught to approach problems analytically or to be consciously aware of the essential steps necessary for the achievement of an effective solution. As a result, when first reading a case you might experience difficulty in imagining what has happened and miss significant points. Again, this is not unusual but it can be demoralising.

It is also usual for a person's thinking to be confused and impulsive when confronted with several aspects of a new problem. If the case situation is unfamiliar, this might be compounded by feelings of inadequacy, of not knowing where to begin. It helps to recognise that this is a normal reaction but, if not anticipated, it can be particularly threatening for someone used to a position of authority, of being the person expected by others to take the initiative.

Some people are natural decision makers but this ability needs to be directed along the lines suggested earlier to be the most effective. Those who do not make decisions so readily should take heart from the fact that well grounded decision making is based upon techniques which can be learnt, and then turned into skills with practice. As mentioned earlier, this practice can be alone or with a group.

Studying alone

If you are studying alone, you will have both advantage and disadvantage.

When an examination has to be prepared for you will gain. Not having been used to the prop of group support should mean that you have greater self reliance – essential in the examination room and indeed in real life since decision making is often a lonely process.

You will lose the benefit of interaction with others in case study sessions and the sparking of ideas that one experiences in group discussion – not that these are always pleasurable occasions as you will read later.

Studying with a group

There are distinct advantages to be gained from studying with a group, provided that you also work alone in order to acquire self confidence in handling cases and self sufficiency in generating ideas.

You can expect support especially if the case is being dealt with in syndicates. Frequently, an element of competition arises between these subgroups and it is amazing how in such circumstances a group will close ranks and protect its own members.

Discussion should be stimulating, with the ideas of one person sparking off those of another. On the other hand, it is also possible to sit back and let others comment without making much effort yourself or even being concerned about your total absence of ideas! In this respect alone a group can be very useful. It will allow you to get along without much preparation. If you debate points made by others or use the ploy of analysing one issue in detail, you can appear very knowledgeable. This is certainly useful in an emergency when you have not had time for preparation but is definitely not recommended. The result is superficial participation. In studying cases, you undoubtedly reap according to how you sow and if you have not given much thought to a case you will not get much out of it. Unlike traditional methods of learning, you cannot reckon on catching up at a later date so lost opportunities are gone for ever.

Conflict and compromise

A very real value of case work in a group setting derives from the interaction of its members and the opportunities you have, as a result of familiarity with the case, to engage in discussion. Better still if this becomes an experience, ie if you become immersed in the case sufficiently to feel something about it, then real and lasting learning is likely to take place – learning, moreover, which will transfer to future problem solving.

This involvement does, however, underline the theme 'Don't expect it to be easy'. Far from it. Expect it at times to be traumatic! Group discussion between involved people is often the opposite of cocoon-like. Ideas clash and a supportive setting very quickly turns into a threatening one. You soon realise how easily conflict develops over decisions even when, as in case study work, the decisions will not be implemented.

You will find it necessary to develop and exercise interpersonal skills in many ways. You have to learn to compromise, to be quiet when you have something really pressing to say, and to handle different roles within the group such as mediator, facilitator and leader. None of this is easy but it is all good experience,

Lack of guidance

In studying cases you might feel abandoned even when supported by the group. In fact there may be occasions when the whole group feels abandoned, as indeed they have been in the sense that their expectations of the lecturer as the person normally looked to for guidance are not being met.

Traditionally, anyone joining a course expects to be 'taught'. This does not happen in case study work and it is bewildering. You do not know what to do or where to begin. You are not told what the problems are, and not only do you have to isolate them for yourself but you are required to come up with solutions to them as well! The usual notes and explanations are missing and, although the fear of putting forward a 'wrong' answer is to some extent removed, there is no reward for a 'right' one because it does not exist.

Not only is it bewildering, it is irritating and you might well ask 'What do we come here for, isn't the lecturer supposed to provide us with solutions and explanations?' In case study work, initially the answer is 'No' although such explanations might come later or be interspersed with the work.

To understand this it has to be appreciated that learning is more important than teaching and that a joint attack on a problem can be of far greater value than a lecture. In case study, the role of the lecturer as a facilitator rather than as the provider of definitive solutions is best appreciated when you have come to terms with the fact that there is generally no single correct 'answer' to be given. After analysing a case, there are usually a number of possibilities from which must be chosen the one which appears to be the most appropriate in the circumstances described. Herein lies another difficulty.

Lack of information

There are only the circumstances set down in the text to work upon. In a real situation so much more is known of the background and, perhaps more important, of how people might be expected to react. This lack of detail is something which many find so difficult to cope with that they seek reprieve by complaining vigorously or by saying that they cannot hope to resolve the case problem without more details. But where does such a request for detail stop? Even in the most detailed case there is never enough information about the organisation, the people or the problem.

Lack of information is something we all have to cope with and it is not unusual. Even in real life, rarely is all the information desired at hand, and to gather it may cost too much or take too long to make it worthwhile to do so. Admittedly, lack of information is more acute in the studying of a case but it is a realistic limitation since real life decisions do have to be made based upon incomplete information.

Quite often you will find that, upon further examination, cases yield more information than is at first apparent. Certainly this is so when tables, charts and graphs are included. Analysing them can be time well spent not only in the information this provides in itself but in the clues it often yields as to the underlying problem.

Lack of information arises in another sense. What are you left with at the end of a case study session? Quite often not much that is tangible. If you have participated fully you are unlikely to have had time to write lecture type notes and you cannot make notes from a textbook.

Do resist feeling anxious over those empty pages. The experience of the case study session will have become part of you in a way that notes never can, no matter how much time you give to studying them. Agreed, they are a prop but what is their real value in a problem situation? You cannot say 'Just a minute I must look up my notes!' Only real learning, internalised learning, is of use in the real world, and studying cases will provide you with many opportunities for this.

10 What can you expect to gain?

We are living in a fast moving, changing world and the familiar rapidly becomes unfamiliar. Work and the environment in which it is carried out is unlikely to remain constant. Some jobs will disappear, others be created and retraining become necessary. A soundly based knowledge of analysis and decision making skills which can be universally applied will never become obsolete and, moreover, is likely to be required to an increasing extent.

These analysis and problem solving skills are fostered in case study work. Because it is the nearest simulation to work place learning, it forms a bridge between theory and practice and a means of developing the analytical, creative and social skills you need both at work and in private life.

The practice that working on cases gives in analysing situations, identifying problems, assessing possible courses of action and deciding priorities not only strengthens these skills but will give you confidence in your ability to cope with difficulties in all aspects of real life.

Awareness and familiarisation with problems

You cannot solve a problem if you have not recognised it as such. Even then things may not be what they seem. A problem which appears on the surface to be simple often turns out to be more complex upon examination. As mentioned in an earlier chapter, an essential first step in analysis is to isolate the root problem. You will find that this detective type of work is excellent training in creating an awareness of cause and effect and a healthy scepticism about apparently straightforward matters.

A fair criticism of cases is that they cannot replace personal experience, nor can they provide familiarity with all possible situations which might arise in the future. However, the same types of problem do tend to re-occur. Details will differ but if when faced with real life problems you recognise similarities to cases you have dealt with, this will not only help you to find a solution but will reduce the anxiety which arises from dealing with the unfamiliar. Indeed, the more familiar you become with handling problem situations the less they should worry you. Furthermore, practice is a means of building up a conceptual framework and as a result when problems arise your thinking reactions should be easier, quicker and more effective.

Analytical skills

Assessing what is likely to be the real source of trouble in a situation is not easy but it is essential since difficulties have to be understood before effective action can be taken. This involves studying all the facts and distinguishing between what are merely symptoms and what looks like the cause itself. You then have to decide what further information is required and if, from whom, or where it can be obtained. Armed with all the information available you then try to understand the situation described.

Problems and symptoms, causes and effects, and situations and principles are frequently entwined in a case. These have to be unravelled by organising the information just as you should in a work setting. The additional difficulty at work is that you are often in the middle of the situation, being pressured from all sides to do something about it immediately. The pace, mental clutter and constraints of real life thus limit opportunities for dealing with problems objectively. In contrast, the relatively sheltered exploring of a case allows you to develop your skills and to examine issues from the outside without the pressure of personal involvement and responsibility.

Decision making skills

Case study work develops and makes use of the capacity to recognise and take account not only of key facts and the significant relationships between them but also of the influence of environmental factors. In handling a case, it becomes apparent that problems do not exist in a vacuum and a broad view has to be taken. This increases the awareness that real life problems have also to be looked at from a broader perspective.

Case study work requires you to sum up situations in a down to earth manner and to use judgment practically in order to produce realistic, effective courses of action. Therefore, these skills are exercised and should improve.

Flexibility of thinking grows from seeing that different solutions are often possible for any one problem. Insight into the different ways in which others approach problems is acquired.

Experimenting with and trying out theories which have been learnt can be done relatively painlessly and without cost. Decision making skills involving the ability to ask the right questions and understand a situation as it is, and not as you would like it to be, improve with practice. Effectiveness in considering and correctly evaluating likely consequences of decisions is increased.

Clearer thinking

Even when identifying with a case you can remain detached and thus be able to view it without the mental blinkers that can hinder real life thinking. Because of this there is less likelihood of possible distortion and all sides of the question are more readily seen.

In a group situation you might be obliged to defend, evaluate, compare and revise your ideas. This necessitates clear thinking. As a result, deciding between courses of action, approaches, methods and procedures becomes easier. Admittedly, you might have to handle assumptions and reach decisions based on incomplete evidence but this is what happens in reality.

Awareness of attitudes

Group analysis particularly heightens sensitivity to the reactions of other people. To gain the most from this you need to be socially perceptive and aware of how attitudes influence and distort decision making.

Cases built around ethical and moral issues are illuminating in this respect. As a result of the thought and discussion arising from such a case, you might feel impelled to question not only the attitudes and value judgments of others but your own as well. In so doing self honesty is rewarded. At least if you are conscious of your beliefs you should find it easier to be objective in your judgments.

Communication skills

An important part of working on a case is the presentation of a 'solution'. It is thus necessary to review your findings and select the best means of presenting them. Communicating ideas clearly and concisely so that others understand is vital to success in gaining their acceptance in any situation. Doing so persuasively but tactfully requires practice and group case work provides this. It also becomes necessary for the views of other people to be listened to with attention and this is a frequently neglected communication skill.

Interpersonal skills

The group setting is one in which interpersonal skills can be practised but do not expect this always to be comfortable. You are in an exposed position personally and professionally when the feasibility of your ideas are to be tested by group opinion. This is especially so when others hold strong views, but there is the bonus of being able to experiment with ideas and have them evaluated without having to live with the consequences.

Challenge from the group helps you to gain not only insight into business operations but also understanding about yourself and a sensitivity and greater awareness of the feelings of others. If an appreciation of their motives can also be acquired, it becomes easier to see how problems arise. Hopefully this can be applied to avoiding them at future times.

There is a great deal that can be gained by closely observing and sensitively responding to the reactions of other people. The more insight is developed into how they feel and react in certain circumstances the more this can be applied in real life at moments when being able to judge a situation quickly and behave appropriately is vital. Further, you stand to gain an appreciation of the wide range of human relationship difficulties which arise in organisations and in private life and a means of learning how to cope with them with at least some degree of understanding.

Shared experience

In order to make judgments and decisions, particularly under conditions of uncertainty, all the information and ideas which can be gathered helps to clear the picture. Through handling cases you begin to realise that such information comes to us in different forms and from many sources, not least from fellow students.

Group case analysis provides frequent opportunities to observe the correct and incorrect use of various techniques, both social and task related. Constructive criticism from others plus self honesty in assessing your own techniques can lead to improvement. Thinking responsibly and responsively will increase your capacity to appreciate how difficulties arise and what can be done to alleviate or prevent them in the future.

Discussions encourage spontaneous comments which might on the surface appear to be offbeat but such comments can spark off more realistic ideas from others. The immensity of the total experience of the members of a group is not always appreciated because for much of the time it is dormant. Case problems act as catalysts in freeing people to share their experiences and so learn from one another.

In a nutshell

Studying cases is different from other forms of learning. Theories which have been learnt are tried out in realistic situations and this results in permanent learning which can be applied more readily to real problems. It is also different in that it demands more than an academic approach. It is difficult not to become involved to some extent and certainly desirable that you should. In this way you experience the situations and learn to cope with them. Some of this experience will be good – occasions when you can explore ideas and feelings and apply knowledge in an interesting and realistic manner. Some will not be good – occasions when you will be obliged to seriously question your attitudes; when others do not agree with you; and aggression, yours as well as theirs, has to be coped with. But good or bad you will be learning more effectively:

a   to analyse a situation including the evaluating of information and searching for problem causes which are not immediately apparent.

b   to acknowledge that others have tenable points of view, defending your own and evaluating one against the other.

c   to rely on your own ability and that of your group to reason through a problem rather than have the solution given to you.

d   to make decisions based on less than complete information by applying problem solving techniques.

e   to communicate the results of your decision making clearly and persuasively.

Part 2   Case studies

Introduction

Part 1 of this book introduced you to case study skills and, by means of skill developments, suggested opportunities for putting these skills into practice. A number of cases now follow which can be used for further practice in building up your expertise. Notes are included with the first few, after which you are on your own – as indeed you must expect to be at some stage of your case study work.

The cases chosen are representative of those devised by the examining boards who currently set external case study examinations, plus a few from individual writers which serve as an example of what you might expect from college staff. This college devising of cases is common for internally set examinations, for example, for the Business and Technician Education Council and for use in courses.

If you have mastered the skills outlined in Part 1 you should be able to make a good attempt at analysing the cases regardless of whether or not you are familiar with the situations. There is a universality about problems which applies to real life as well as to cases, and a firm based logical approach to solving them is a skill which will never be redundant.

The meter scheme

Midborough Council offices housed a number of local authority departments in a main building and an assortment of neighbouring, prefabricated huts. All of the departments made use of a centrally located
photocopying machine. Staff needing copies made them as required,
entering the number of copies made, and their department, in a log book
kept by the machine. The copier was situated in an alcove in a main
corridor. There were no other reprographic facilities within the Council
offices. Reprographic work beyond the scope of the photocopier was
produced externally.

The increasing use made of the machine, together with the rapid rise in
paper costs had resulted in the whole question of copying expenditure
being drawn to the attention of the newly appointed chief executive.
Analysis of the log book and comparison with the total copies recorded on
the counter built into the machine, indicated that only about 60 per cent of
the copies made were actually being recorded in the log book. Hence, the
extent of each department's usage of the machine was not accurately
known.

After discussion of the problem with departmental heads, it was decided
to have the copying machine modified so that it could only be operated if a
small, plug-in meter was inserted in the control unit. A meter was issued
to each departmental head, and members of staff requiring copies had to
collect the meter from their departmental head's office. They were also
required to enter brief details of the nature and number of copies made in
a separate, departmental log book, and initial each entry.

A number of shortcomings of the scheme soon became apparent. It was
a considerable inconvenience to collect and return the meter to the head's
office, especially in the more widely dispersed departments. Quite often,
staff arrived at the office to collect the meter, only to find that someone had
already taken it. It sometimes happened, too, that people did not return
the meter promptly after use, and this was a further source of aggravation.
Furthermore, there still did not appear to be an accurate correlation
between meter readings and log book entries.

However, it did become apparent that the copying machine was used
mainly by three departments, each of which accounted for 25 to 30 per
cent of total usage. The remaining departments were infrequent users of
the machine.

The chief executive had been made aware of the shortcomings of the 'meter' scheme, and was considering how best the departmental heads might exercise control over copying costs, but at the same time avoid the inconvenience and frustrations which the meter scheme engendered.

NB The small plug-in meters incorporated a digital counter which recorded the number of copies made by users of the individual meters. In addition, the total number of copies produced on the machine was recorded by the non-removable counter built into the machine.

Question 1

What do you consider to be the central problem in this situation? Write this down briefly before reading further.

Now read the following. Does your assessment of the situation correspond with any of the statements *a* to *f* below?

a Employees are using the copying machine for their own private purposes.
b Copying costs are increasing.
c Employees are becoming increasingly frustrated by the shortcomings of the meter scheme.
d Employees are not following laid-down procedures.
e There is a need to exercise control over copying costs and reduce inconvenience and frustration caused by the meter scheme.
f The chief executive should not be concerning himself with minor problems of this kind.
g Some other issue is more important in this situation?

Comment, discussion and further questions on these alternatives are given in the corresponding paragraphs in the commentary section which follows.

Commentary

a **Employees are using the copying machine for their own private purposes**

There is no direct evidence in the case to indicate that employees are using the copying machine for their own private purposes, although, of course, this may be so. Perhaps this assumption is based on your own personal experience in a similar situation.

Suppose a series of random checks indicated that about 10 per cent of copying was for non-business purposes. What action would you take as chief executive? What reaction would you expect as a result? If the 'private' copying was 5 per cent would you take the same action? If only 2 per cent? Think about the implications of your answer.

b **Copying costs are increasing**

This seems to be the case, and indeed prompted the introduction of the meter scheme in the first place. However, the scheme has obvious shortcomings, and there is no indication in the case that it has, in fact, reduced the amount of copying being done. Does the chief executive see a reduction in copying costs as his main objective in this situation? If not, what are his objectives?

c **Employees are becoming increasingly frustrated by the shortcomings of the meter scheme**

Employees are clearly frustrated by aspects of the scheme, although we are not told that their frustration is *increasing*. What is causing this frustration? Is it simply that they sometimes have difficulty in getting hold of the meter? What did the introduction of the meters imply in terms of managements' attitude to employees? Is it possible to assess the 'cost' to the organisation of employee frustration in situations of this kind?

d **Employees are not following laid-down procedures**

Why is it that people sometimes fail to adhere to set procedures? Is it intentional, a wilful refusal to work to rules or because the procedure has not been adequately explained to them? Perhaps they do not understand the procedure, or do not believe that it is needed. Where a new procedure is causing problems, perhaps people find it difficult to get used to it in place of a long-established and familiar routine. To what extent does prior discussion with all concerned of a proposed change improve its chance of successful implementation? Might this have helped with the meter scheme, or does the scheme have inherent failings anyway? Do you think that consultation on an issue of this kind would be an unnecessary waste of time?

e **There is a need to exercise control over copying costs and reduce inconvenience and frustration caused by the meter scheme**

This is what we are told the chief executive wanted to achieve (final paragraph of case). From his point of view this is the way he wishes to resolve the problem. What precisely do you think the chief executive means by his use of the word 'control'? What does the word control mean to you?

f The chief executive should not be concerning himself with minor problems of this kind

Why do you consider this to be a minor problem? What information within the case leads you to this conclusion? What kinds of problem should a chief executive become personally involved with? Just how bad is this meter scheme problem? Who should deal with it?

g Some other issue is more important in this situation

You may consider that one or more of the following issues are more important than those listed above:

- the use of shared resources and the problem of apportioning costs among the various users
- geographically dispersed staff coming to a central service point
- no single department appears to have responsibility for the machine

The issues considered important will depend largely upon the viewpoint adopted. Is the viewpoint you are using based upon your own work experience, or are you putting yourself in the position of one of the participants in the situation described? Try to submerge yourself in the case situation and consider what it would mean to you then.

Have you already decided what might be done to remedy this situation? Question 1 asks only that you consider what is the central problem.

When we are asked to analyse a situation, there is a temptation not simply to analyse it, but to decide almost at once what should be done about it.

We tend to take the first solution to the problem that appears to have a reasonable chance of success.

The way in which we define a problem strongly influences the type of solution we propose for its resolution.

If time allows, it is usually worth while delaying the search for solutions until we have explored the problem fully and are quite sure we understand all its facets.

It is also useful to consider several possible solutions, rather than one, and to weigh up which of these is likely to achieve most of the desired outcome.

Question 2

Now that you have thought about the situation and the problems it contains, what action could you recommend to the chief executive to improve matters? Write down your suggestions before reading on.

Now read the following. Do your recommendations correspond with any of these points?

a   Abandon the meter scheme altogether and return to the earlier 'open-access' policy. Place the onus on departmental heads to keep copying within reasonable bounds.
b   Appoint a machine operator through whom all departmental copying will be channelled.
c   Issue each employee who needs to use the machine with his own personal meter, and monitor usage at departmental level.
d   Agree on a copying budget for each department and expect each departmental head to ensure that his department keeps within it.
e   Obtain further information before recommending any course of action.
f   None of these.

For questions and comments on these alternative recommendations refer to the appropriate paragraphs in the Commentary section which follows.

Commentary

a   **Abandon the meter scheme altogether and return to the earlier 'open-access' policy. Place the onus on departmental heads to keep copying within reasonable bounds**

If this is done, how might each individual department head keep his subordinates' copying within reasonable bounds? What does 'reasonable' mean? What would be the implications for the chief executive in abandoning the meter scheme?

b   **Appoint a machine operator through whom all departmental copying will be channelled**

What are the advantages of this proposal? Are there any disadvantages? What desirable objectives would this proposal achieve?

Would the operator vet material to eliminate unnecessary copying? Would you expect the operator to decide on what was unauthorised or unnecessary work? How would the operator decide on this? What authority would the operator have? What would be the implications of that?

Would the mere fact that an operator had been appointed in itself deter people from making unnecessary requests for copying?

c **Issue each employee who needs to use the machine with his own personal meter and monitor usage on a departmental basis**

Are there any disadvantages in this idea? Have you asked yourself what the likely cost would be of providing the additional meters? How might usage be monitored within the various departments? Assuming that individual usage was recorded regularly in each department, how might departmental heads make use of this information? Would this information be sufficient to make this recommendation effective?

d **Agree on a copying budget for each department and expect each departmental head to ensure that his department keeps within it**

It would seem sensible to think about how much copying is needed by the various departments. There is no indication in the case that any thought has been given to this aspect of the situation. Only if this is done can a budget be agreed. This would then provide a yardstick against which each department's copying costs could be compared. Any significant deviation from the budget would prompt questions as to the reasons.

There are still a number of potential difficulties however. Is knowledge of his department's copying costs, received at regular intervals, all the departmental head needs to know in order to keep within his budget?

e **Obtain further information before recommending any course of action**

It is usually worthwhile considering the information that is available in dealing with any situation of this kind. Have you considered what further information you would seek in this particular situation? Would you expect this kind of information to have been available in this instance? Obtainable at relatively low costs? Time and cost will be incurred in collecting information. It is always worth considering what difference the information you are seeking is likely to make to your understanding of a situation, and whether, as a result, its collection is worth the cost.

Some further information on the situation is given on page 83.

Data based upon random surveys carried out over a representative period of 2 weeks

Machine running approx $4\frac{1}{4}$ hours per day
Available for use $7\frac{1}{2}$ hours per day
Copying speed: 8 copies per minute
Cost per copy: 3p (total costs averaged over number of copies produced)

Does this additional information help you to decide an appropriate course of action?

Is this information useful as it stands or do you need to manipulate it in some way to make it more useful?

Having considered this information what course of action would you now recommend? If it is one of the alternatives *a–f* refer to the appropriate paragraphs for further questions and discussion.

f **None of these**

Perhaps you have an alternative recommendation. There are several possibilities. What are the advantages of your recommendation over those discussed above? Does it have any disadvantages?

Ask yourself the following questions in relation to your recommendation:

1 What objectives will it achieve? Does it meet the chief executive's objective of 'exercising control over copying costs, but at the same time avoid the inconvenience and frustrations' of the existing scheme? What does 'exercise control' mean?

2 What tangible savings are likely to result? What will it cost to implement? Will it be simple to operate, easy to understand, be acceptable to employees?

Question 3

What do you think the chief executive means by 'exercising control over copying costs'? Is the word 'control' appropriate here? Does he simply want to reduce costs or stabilise costs?

What do you understand by the phrase 'exercising control over copying costs'?

Make a few notes on your interpretation of these words before reading on.

Commentary

Control – the word control implies regulation, achieving and/or maintaining a desired state.

In order to exercise control, certain basic requirements have to be satisfied. These are as follows:

a   There has to be an agreed or stated standard, target, output, budget, condition, etc which it is desired to maintain.
b   It has to be possible to measure or determine the actual level of performance, output or condition being achieved at any time.
c   If the actual performance, output or condition differs from that required, means must be available for correcting the deviation.

In the case study there is concern expressed about increasing copying costs, but no indication that anyone has considered how much copying is really necessary. Until this is done, however tentatively, control is not possible. Reduction in copying can be achieved in various ways but this does not constitute 'control'.

We do not know in the situation described whether the volume of copying is rising or costs are simply rising as a result of inflation.

On the basis of this discussion, can you now decide on a course of action to recommend to the chief executive? In doing so, consider the cost in the broadest meaning of that term, of implementing your proposal and compare this with the benefits you anticipate. Unless the benefits more than offset the cost, is the proposal worth implementing?

Try a few simple calculations using the data given in paragraph 2*e*.

The total monthly copying costs are:

$$£(4.25 \times 60 \times 8 \times 20) \times \frac{3p}{100} = £1224$$

(assuming 20 working days per month)

If cost reduction is a major objective of your proposal (and there may well be other important objectives) consider what proportion of these total monthly costs your scheme might save and what it would cost to implement and maintain your scheme in order to achieve this saving.

A question of training

Introduction – the company

Thomas Henderson & Co Ltd is a firm employing some 2500 in the engineering industry. The main products are engineering components and a wide range of hand tools, which are sold for use both within industry and for the domestic handyman market.

The company was established by Thomas Henderson in 1858 and the family still retain the controlling interest in the firm. Charles Henderson, a man in his early seventies is the present chairman and his son John, aged 39 is the managing director. Both father and son have followed a family tradition of working up through the firm and while Charles Henderson is an engineer by training his son John made his mark as one of the best salesmen the company has ever had.

While the company has a long-established national reputation and a good brand image, pressure of costs in an inflationary situation have forced its trade customers to look closely at Henderson's price competitiveness. In the domestic market, many shops also stock cheaper hand tools. These products, while they may be of inferior quality, present a serious challenge to the company.

Henderson's main offices and factory are situated in the Midlands. Regional offices for sales and distribution are located in London, Bristol, Glasgow, Cardiff, Newcastle and Liverpool. Marketing policy and general sales policies are controlled by the managing director, although the functional responsibility is held by Edward Hyde-Smith, the marketing director, who started with the firm as a salesman in Bristol, some fifteen years previously.

The personnel department

A small central personnel department is located at head office. On the staff side its functions mainly concern wage and salary administration. Formally, the department has the overall responsibility for recruitment and training, but in practice it only handles the arrangements for recruitment, all decisions being taken by line managers. There is consultation with the managing director on more senior appointments. The personnel manager,

Joe Ferguson, is a former regional sales manager of the company. He has been with Henderson's for some thirty years and is now nearing retirement.

The overall problem

The Board of Henderson's has become conscious that the rate of turnover among their salesmen is high enough to cause concern. The Board are also worried about the apparent need to buy management talent from outside the company. The following situations can be isolated.

1 The graduate turnover problem

Henderson's has recently decided that it needs to improve its management by offering a few places each year to business studies graduates or Business and Technician Education Council Higher National Diploma holders, from universities or polytechnics, who want to make a career in either marketing or finance. In the case of marketing entrants, after a two-week spell at head office, graduates are expected to work in a regional office for some time, gaining practical sales and sales administration experience. However, the turnover rate is rather high: out of four entrants each year, three have left within two years, one on average within the first six months.

A recent case was that of Jim Tovey, a Business and Technician Education Council Higher National Diploma holder from Franchester Polytechnic. On entering the firm, after his initial two-week tour of the various departments at head office he worked on sales administration, spending almost all of his time checking invoices and salesmen's expense sheets. During the next six months he was engaged on fact finding about possible retail outlets. It was felt that this year was necessary before he could be used as a representative. Besides, it was argued, the basic clerical and administrative work had to be done by someone. Jim Tovey did not wait to see what sales experience was like, he applied for a marketing job with another company in the pharmaceutical field. After appropriate training he was given a territory to operate. He is happy in his new job and his sales record, his former colleagues hear, is a good one.

2 The ineffective salesman

Fred Bayliss entered Henderson's in his mid-twenties as a regional representative based in Cardiff. He seemed on recruitment to be an energetic man, but possessed no previous sales experience having worked in clerical jobs hitherto. He was allocated a territory and given a company car. After an initial briefing he was left mainly to his own devices. The regional sales manager was very busy and only seemed to have time for numerous meetings and periodic checks of sales figures. After six months the regional sales manager reported to head office that sales were noticeably down in Fred Bayliss' territory and that his performance was poor compared to other salesmen in the region. Admittedly they were experienced men, but surely good salesmen had it in them to succeed and Fred did not appear to have this innate ability. The sales manager recommends replacing Fred, if his sales results do not significantly improve within three months.

3 The problem of management succession

Henderson's are worried about creating a source of internal recruitment for senior management positions. In recent years the company has had to buy talent from outside, feeling that existing personnel were not up to more responsibility. The graduate training scheme was part of this policy.

Naturally enough, existing staff were unhappy with poor promotion prospects, morale was affected and some able younger men left the company. It was decided to try the experiment of sending Don Markham, an outstanding marketing executive, a former graduate trainee and then in his late twenties, to study for a Master in Business Administration qualification at the London Business School. Don Markham gained this qualification and came back to Henderson's brimming over with enthusiasm. He resumed his previous job, with additional responsibilities for long-range planning, and received a small salary increase. After three months, Don left the company for a much better-paid attractive middle-management job with prospects of promotion, in another engineering company. The Board felt let down by this episode and were reinforced in their distrust of outside training for their own personnel.

Having read the case, now assume that you are a newly appointed personnel officer who has been asked to investigate the company's personnel policies in general and the above three aspects in particular and in a report to Mr Ferguson, personnel manager:

a State what the problems were in each of these cases.
b Suggest how the situations could have been avoided.
c Outline a suitable training programme for people in these categories.
d Make overall recommendations for a long term solution to their personnel problems.

Notes on Thomas Henderson & Co Ltd

Here are the case writers' notes indicating points you might have made in your report. How did you fare? Did you make other points? Do you disagree with any of those given here?

In evaluating a report such as this, the correct format and an appropriate tone would be important considerations. Considerable tact would be needed in expressing criticism of the current practices including the lack of experience and capability of the present personnel manager.

The situation in general

The problems have arisen because of a lack of clear personnel and training policy within the company. It is evident that the personnel manager has a low status within the firm and is assisted by a small department that concentrates on routine administration. The real power of decision lies elsewhere – ultimately with the chairman and the managing director. Neither of these men have a clear idea of the purpose and function of training but are obviously concerned about the present situation.

How could the individual situations have been avoided?

1 The graduate turnover problem

There is no point in recruiting a young man with good academic qualifications unless the company can provide a stimulating and challenging introduction to sales work. Jim Tovey should have been given full sales training and then put out on the road. After initial experience he should then have been sent on more advanced sales management courses to improve both his techniques and his administrative knowledge. Boredom and a lack of stimulus leads to poor work and a desire by the more energetic man for a change of job. However, the new entrant should be made aware that efficient routine procedures, eg invoicing, are also part of any well run firm.

2 The ineffective salesman

This was a classic case of poor initial training, inadequate follow-up and ineffective supervision. When his performance was not up to standard, the salesman, Fred Bayliss, was blamed for this not the management for creating the situation. Note the belief of the sales manager that good salesmen are born not made. This shows an underlying disbelief in the value of training and not much grasp of the need for encouragement and regular supervision.

3 The problem of management succession

Many firms send promising managers on high-powered courses of this nature. This is all very well, but the experiment is almost certainly doomed to failure if the man is not used properly when he returns. Naturally, the returning manager feels that he should be promoted and gain salary, status and a fresh challenge. The firm provided insufficiently for those needs – it did not really know what to do with Don Markham. Inevitably the investment was wasted, and the bright young man went elsewhere where his talent was likely to be better used and appreciated. The moral here is, do not raise expectations in managers that you cannot fulfil either through lack of imagination or the lack of job opportunities in the smaller company.

Suitable training programme

1 The graduate entrant

a A one-week induction programme: general outline of the company and its objectives, tour of departments, information on products and processes.
b Two weeks' basic sales training.
c Six months' field experience.
d One-week sales representative course.
e A further six months' field experience.

In his second year the graduate should progress to a marketing programme at head office, including market research, advertising and sales administration. A definite job should be allocated at this stage – the trainee status being replaced by a recognised management position.

2 Salesman's training

a A one-week induction course: introduction to company structure and its overall objectives, acquisition of product knowledge.
b Two-week sales representative course: concentrating on techniques of selling and administrative skills required by a representative in order to be fully effective.
c Periodic refresher courses as for all salesmen. During the first year, attach the new salesman to an experienced man for advice and assistance as a counsellor.

3 The experienced manager

No formal training is required in this case. The man has learnt theoretical approaches and high-level techniques in his MBA course. The Board should appoint him to a middle-management post with firm arrangements for his succeeding in a short time a senior manager nearing retirement.

During this period, special projects and assignments should be given to make use of his abilities and retain his interest. A salary increment should be a significant not nominal one and be linked to a senior job specification.

Overall long term recommendations

The company requires:

a To establish its training aims, ensure that expenditure is properly channelled and that a coherent policy is followed. The suggested training programmes and analysis of previous situations makes this point. The company also needs to review all existing personnel policies.

b A replacement to the existing personnel manager (soon to retire) should be sought. A professionally qualified and experienced senior personnel man is required. It is suggested that an eventual seat on the Board should be considered. The company needs to place more emphasis on the personnel function. The new manager should be responsible for all personnel work, including manual employees. He would report directly to the managing director.

c A training officer should be appointed at head office with overall responsibility for this function. His brief would include looking for suitable internal promotable staff, designing training programmes, supervising trainees, running internal courses for all levels of staff and arranging for staff to go on suitable externally run courses. The training officer would report to the personnel manager.

d All managers should be made aware of the value of training and the cost of wastage. This responsibility should be written into managers' job specifications.

e New entrants to the company, whether recent graduates or older men, should for their first year be linked to an experienced employee who would be given specific responsibility for guidance and advice. Training is not just a matter of courses attended but also of daily guidance and advice when required.

Edano Chemical Co Ltd

John Davidson (52) had worked for Edano for 10 years as general manager of a small foreign subsidiary which was engaged in work of a highly technical nature. He was fortunate in having as second-in-command an extremely efficient administrative manager who virtually ran the company. This left Davidson free to deal with any complex technical problems, which he did expertly and from which he derived a great deal of satisfaction.

Even though Davidson was aware that Edano had suffered economic setbacks it was still a shock when the company decided to sell out its foreign interests and he was recalled to the UK. This coincided with the retirement of the assistant general manager of one of Edano's larger branches, a post he was asked to fill.

The job included deputising for the general manager during his frequent absences on business and a great deal of work concerned with the day-to-day running of the company. Davidson's desk was frequently piled high with files and, being a thorough and conscientious person, he regularly took a briefcase full of work home.

He thought of himself primarily as a technical expert and responded favourably when a member of the sales department began to seek advice on technical matters raised by customers. This person welcomed the interest shown and, since he lacked experience and was pleased to receive the benefit of Davidson's expertise, took his problems to him regularly. Before long, however, Davidson began to deal with the customers himself over technical matters since he judged himself to be the most competent to do so. As a result, customers frequently contacted him direct instead of working through the sales department.

In his previous post, Davidson had been used to hand drafting his reports and letters because of the highly technical nature of their contents. He continued to do so, rarely dictating to his secretary. Because he was a stickler for checking facts and constantly revised and corrected, he used a great deal of paper. On the Friday before the Spring Bank Holiday when he planned to take a considerable amount of work home he was told that there were no sheets of paper available. He marched straight out of his office to see the administrative manager who operated a system of ordering the stationery as and when it appeared to be necessary. Davidson ticked him off soundly stating that he personally would check the stock and place an order for a 12 month's supply which would ensure that the situation did not arise again. Although the administrative manager was upset over the incident, nevertheless he was glad to get rid of what he regarded as a rather boring job.

Not long after this, Davidson put in a request for an assistant as he felt himself to be overworked. The request was passed on to head office but was refused on the grounds that there were sufficient heads of department for specialist tasks and his role did not warrant an assistant. Davidson had no alternative but to accept this. He did, however, alter the holiday rota so as to take only two out of the five weeks' annual leave which he was shortly to commence.

When the general manager heard of this he ordered him to take the full time due and said that upon his recommendation to head office Davidson was to be promoted to a research post elsewhere in the organisation when he returned from leave.

Question

Analyse this case, identifying examples of poor management practice and personnel policy.

Notes on Edano Chemical Co Ltd

Paragraph 1

John Davidson not only delegated, he abdicated!

Paragraph 2

An example of thinking only in terms of filling a vacant post and not of selecting the right person for the job. Short term expediency is rarely a means to long term efficiency. Apparently, the company failed to prepare Davidson for the possibility of his return to the UK or to confer with him concerning his new post.

Paragraph 3

Davidson was clearly a square peg in a round hole, did not receive the necessary coaching from his superior and was not coping well with the new demands upon him. Did he delegate sufficiently? He was not familiar with the daily routine – see paragraph 1.

Paragraph 4

Why were staff required to deal with technical matters beyond their knowledge? Implications for training here. Davidson was usurping the sales manager's authority and encouraging the chain of command and communication to be ignored both internally and externally.

Paragraph 5

Davidson's secretary's shorthand skill was not being used and she was likely to resent doing little more than copy typing. Hand drafting was a great waste of time. Why was there no stationery control system which could have been operated by a junior member of staff and would have avoided an out-of-stock position? Davidson did not handle the administrative manager well. In placing an order for 12 months' stock he demonstrated his ignorance of stock control principles. However the administrative manager regarded any aspect of his responsibilities, he should not have allowed them to be taken from him.

Paragraph 6

No wonder he was overworked, he took on everyone else's job!

Paragraph 7

So Davidson is to end up where he ought to have been placed originally – in a post which will be satisfying to him and in which he can be of the greatest value to the company. However, he must realise that although promoted he is being moved out and he is likely to be bewildered and unhappy. He has after all worked very hard and has tried to pass on his valuable knowledge to anyone who appeared to need it. He might well feel resentful and either leave or become less well motivated.

Many of the incidents could have been avoided had the general manager stepped in earlier. He could have recommended that Davidson's job description be altered so that he was employed in an advisory capacity, in which his expertise would have been valuable, rather than in an executive capacity. It appears likely that the general manager's recommendation for Davidson's transfer is the result of responding to complaints from his departmental managers, but the problem did not appear overnight. His final high handed dealing with the situation is to be deplored and is unlikely to leave him with the respect of any of his staff no matter how strongly they may feel about Davidson.

The distorting mirror

About four years after Tom Hardy had been made production control manager at the West Midlands Machine Company, the superintendent of the company resigned. Mr Miller, works director in charge of manufacturing, discussed with the company's managing director the problem of filling the position and they decided to transfer Hardy from production control manager to superintendent.

The seven foremen in charge of the manufacturing departments reported to the superintendent. It was his job to supervise these foremen in operations, and one of the major requirements of the job was personnel administration. The superintendent reported to Miller.

As production control manager, Hardy had also reported to Miller. Although this job had required merely the setting up of overall production schedules, Hardy had broadened his outlook in his four years in that position. He had studied plant operations and had gained a good understanding of technical production problems, although he had never had actual production experience. Before becoming production control manager, he had been the company's buyer.

Hardy was liked by all the foremen and also by the 400-odd employees in the shop. Both foremen and workmen had come to Hardy with personal problems that ordinarily would have been taken up with the superintendent. It was natural, therefore, that Hardy was transferred to the superintendent's position when it became vacant. Miller, however, who was 50 years old and 10 years Hardy's senior, subsequently came to have some doubts about the move. Miller had been a machinist in his early days with the company and had worked up through the ranks to his position of works director in charge of production. He began to think that Hardy lacked a technical background adequate for the position of superintendent.

After Hardy had been superintendent for several months, friction developed between Hardy and Miller. Miller complained to the managing director that Hardy was opinionated, gave snap judgments and knew little about technical processes.

About a year after Hardy became superintendent, this friction had become more pronounced and was aggravated by pressure of work caused by several important contracts taken on by the company. Miller complained to the managing director that Hardy did not have the technical background necessary to meet the technical problems arising in connection with the new work. The managing director thought Hardy was a valuable man as a personnel administrator, however, and would not agree to dismissing him. Finally, the managing director called in a firm of management consultants to make an organisation study which would include the evaluation of key men. In this way he sought to receive advice from the management consultants as to what action should be taken in the Hardy matter.

The management consultants assigned to the problem spent about two weeks talking informally with each executive and key man down to the rank of assistant foreman. He discussed with each man what his job was; what he depended on other departments or key men for; what difficulties he experienced in executing his job; what types of problems he met; and how he solved them.

During the course of the management consultant's association with Hardy and Miller, each discussed his personal relationships fully on a businesslike basis. Both men had been assured that the management consultant would not use the information in such a way as to cause embarrassment.

The management consultant concluded that Hardy's judgment was excellent and that he had a keen sense of human understanding in dealing with personal problems of his subordinates. His subordinates liked him, and although he did not know all the technical aspects of operations in their departments, they said he was helpful to them in solving technical problems by suggesting possible ways of doing things. Many of these suggestions, they said, were no good but by talking the technical problems over with him they got new ideas. Hardy did not try to force his unworkable ideas on them. They said he was exacting, however, in finding out why an idea was not good and that often in trying to explain why it was impracticable they found that their first reaction was wrong and that the method suggested would work, although they had never tried it before. The foremen said that between Hardy and the methods engineer, whose job it was to design tools and specify methods, they felt they had all the technical assistance they needed.

The management consultant found that Miller was an executive who did a fair job of coordinating the efforts of men reporting to him. The consultant observed that he frequently gave instructions to his subordinates regarding rather minor administrative aspects of their departments. Those reporting to him were the superintendent, the production control manager, the methods engineer, the industrial engineer, the maintenance foreman, the chief inspector and the buyer.

The management consultant was present at many information conferences between Hardy and Miller as they went about their work. He observed that Hardy would analyse a problem in a fraction of the time that it took Miller, and it seemed to the consultant that his judgment was usually better than Miller's even on problems that Miller had thought over prior to presenting them to Hardy. Often Miller would call Hardy to his office and ask him if he did not think they should make a certain move. Hardy would frequently react in a flash and inform Miller immediately why such a move should not be made.

Questions

1 Draw up a personality profile of Tom Hardy *as he sees himself*, ie a self image.
2 Produce a personality profile of Hardy *as seen by Miller*.
3 Produce a personality profile of Hardy *as you see him*.

The Bold House Hotel

After 25 years in retailing, John Bold has realised a long standing ambition in relinquishing his position as a departmental manager in a chain store and buying a small hotel a few miles from the coast in attractive rural surroundings. This he has achieved by means of an inheritance together with the sale of his detached house in the London suburbs which effectively represented his life savings.

The hotel, with 22 twin or double bedrooms, is in good order and pleasantly situated but has been somewhat neglected as a business by the previous owner. Bookings in the financial year 1982/83 showed approximately 30 per cent occupancy. Even in the summer months this rarely exceeded 55 per cent. Being situated in a small village, there is plentiful labour available for full- or part-time work of a hotel or catering nature. In addition to the bedrooms and usual public rooms, there is a flat for the owner/manager and a small suite suitable for a chef or assistant manager. The dining room can seat up to 40 people and an extension to the rear of the hotel provides a large room suitable for wedding receptions, dances or conferences. The latter could seat 150 people cinema style. It is functionally decorated and has no special lighting or conference equipment.

There is a pleasant, comfortably furnished bar.

There is a garden of two-thirds of an acre, part of which is taken up by a car park for about 30 cars.

John and his wife live alone, their two children having married and left home. While they carry no financial responsibilities other than their own livelihoods, they have invested virtually all of their capital in the hotel. Any significant expenditure would have to be raised from revenue or borrowed.

Within the limits of their knowledge and resources the Bolds are eager to make a success of their new venture. Since agreeing to acquire it, they have spent a good deal of time discussing possible ventures and schemes to build up a successful business. Various ideas have emerged and a list of possibilities drawn up as follows:

- establish a high-class restaurant
- use the extension as a discotheque
- establish a residential conference centre
- create a comfortable family hotel

- offer bargain-break weekends at reduced rates
- enlarge the bar and compete with the one local pub
- offer morning coffee and afternoon tea to passing motorists
- create a children's play area in the garden

The new owners are conservative by nature, certainly not used to borrowing large sums of money and totally inexperienced as hoteliers or caterers. John has sensed that they must make some decisions of principle before going much further. He knows that it is not possible to pursue all the identified options and is feeling constrained by not knowing what would be involved in achieving success with some of them.

Question

What advice would you offer?

Western Sausage Co Ltd

Company details

Sausages, sausage meat, pork pies and savouries had been produced at the Pinecombe factory of Western Sausage Co Ltd since it was built in 1907. The factory premises were modernised in 1947 and extended in 1961, but eight years later the owners sold out to a large, national food manufacturer.

After the change in ownership, the Pinecombe factory continued operation as a subsidiary of the main group. Apart from detailed profit plans, production targets and other management controls, there was little direct interference from head office management in the day-to-day running of the Western Sausage Co Ltd.

The factory was managed by a plant manager with a production manager, three foremen and six supervisors to control the 60 production workers. Each worker was paid on a piece-rate basis with appropriate bonus levels. In addition, overtime beyond the 39-hour week was paid at time and one-third on weekdays, and time and one-half on Saturdays. The production workers favoured piece-rates, which they felt provided them with an immediate incentive.

The production manager was also responsible for the packing department, which was controlled by a supervisor and manned by four packers. However, coordination of packing and dispatch involved liaison with the transport manager, who controlled the finished goods, cold store and the company's 10 van drivers.

Quality was satisfactory and was effectively monitored by four food technologists, while all technical and financial matters were the responsibility of the plant manager, who reported to his divisional chief at head office.

The capacity problems

In October 1983, scheduled production of sausages and sausage meat was increased by 20 per cent over the January–June output levels. The plant manager was informed by head office that the rise was to be obtained with no increase in manning beyond the agreed 1983 levels.

The increase in production which resulted from the head office directive caused a backlog of work to build up in the packing department. The supervisor asked the production manager for two additional staff to cope with the situation. This request was passed to the personnel department, who stated that the establishment figures for packing did not allow for any increase in staffing levels. The personnel department consisted of three people – the personnel manager, his secretary and a male clerical worker – and was responsible for the hire and discharge of all labour, welfare, safety, training and departmental manning levels. Any dispute arising in, or between, departments over labour problems were referred to the personnel manager.

The request for two extra packers was eventually referred to the plant manager with the request that a special case be made in view of the sudden increase in production. However, the plant manager stated that he had no authority to increase staff beyond the agreed 1983 levels. He pointed out that the year's budget had been allocated, the packing department was staffed at its correct level of four packers and the head office had specifically stated that the production increase was not to involve any additional labour. He also advised the production manager that any difficulties might be overcome by the redeployment of existing labour.

The packing section was paid standard day-rates, with a half-yearly productivity bonus. The packers liked this system because the level of work in the department varied considerably, and, in addition, the lump sum productivity bonus was paid at two important times of the year: before the annual holidays and the end of the year.

The backlog in packing also caused serious delay for the delivery van drivers, who were paid a basic salary, plus commission on sales. Their late arrival at supermarkets, hotels, shops, restaurants and snack bars resulted in lost sales. To maintain their earnings, the drivers sought alternative outlets, which increased the length of their working day. By late November 1983, the van drivers were threatening to take industrial action unless the problem was resolved.

The production manager tried to persuade several production workers to transfer to packing on a temporary basis. However, the lack of piece-rates, the different levels of skill involved and the colder working conditions (packing was located adjacent to the finished goods cold store) made the offer unattractive to production workers.

Questions

1 Draw an organisation chart showing the line and functional relationships in the company.
2 How would you propose taking 'the heat' out of the present situation?

3 If a reorganisation of employees' duties were required, how could employees be persuaded to adopt new methods of working?
4 Outline the main advantages and disadvantages of the methods of payment at present employed by Western Sausage Co Ltd.
5 The coordination of packing and dispatch involves liaison between the packing supervisor and the transport manager. What is coordination and why is it so important? Are there any disadvantages in the present arrangements?
6 How could you describe the communications processes in Western Sausage Co Ltd? Can you suggest ways in which they might be improved?

Jenkinsons Ltd

Jenkinsons Ltd is a small, family operated, department store situated in Smith Street in a medium sized provincial town. Smith Street runs parallel to the town's Beaton Street, which is a main shopping centre. Originally, Smith Street was the 'exclusive' shopping street. While factory workers and farm hands would use the shops in Beaton Street, their employers would use those in Smith Street.

During the past 20 years, the character of the town has changed. A large industrial estate has been established and several large housing estates have been developed to serve both workers on the industrial estate and as 'dormitory' estates for people working in the two nearby major cities. These developments have produced a massive influx of people to the town and Beaton Street has expanded to cater for their needs – an increased range of shops – major retailers moving in and a general trading-up in terms of the products offered. 'High Street type' retailers have moved into Smith Street and Jenkinsons Ltd is the sole survivor of the 'exclusive' shops.

Jenkinsons consists of five departments: clothing, leatherware (shoes, handbags, cases), cosmetics, lighting fitments and electrical. While few of the products are 'exclusive' in the true sense, they have a significantly higher price than their equivalents in the Beaton Street shops and in return generally offer better quality, more 'classic' designs, less obvious mass production and are not normally available in the Beaton shops. Jenkinsons' has found that these products which appeal to its traditional 'rural elite' customers also appeal to some of the wealthier 'newcomers', particularly those in the 25–35 age group.

The store has not changed much in its basic character over the last 20 years. It regularly receives fresh coats of paint to maintain the smartness of the basically gold and brown decor. While the customer is free to browse among the products, an assistant is always available nearby as the products are arranged on an oblong counter basis for small items and rack or podium display for larger ones. Each counter has an assistant behind it (in the centre of the oblong) and each podium or group of racks has an assistant in attendance. Almost all assistants are female, aged 40 and over. Younger staff tend to be put off by the lower wages compared to Beaton Street shops and the insistence on a basically black 'uniform' (fine knit cardigan, blouse and skirt). The exterior of the shop was 'modernised' 10 years ago when four large windows replaced the existing seven bay windows. At the same time, fluorescent lighting was installed throughout the store.

Jenkinsons is now faced with a major decision. Profits have been declining as its traditional customers found Smith Street a less attractive shopping street as the High Street type retailers moved in. The store would have gone out of existence had it not been for the interest shown in the products by the better off newcomers. The general feeling among these is that 'they like the goods but they don't particularly like the shop'. The managing director feels that they only tap a small share of this market.

A major retailing firm has made a substantial offer for the site occupied by Jenkinsons. The managing director could use this money to relocate the store on a site near to the residential areas favoured by the town-based part of his traditional market. This site is in a very small shopping centre with a delicatessen, haute couture dress shop, antiques' shop and an independent wine merchants.

As he sees it the managing director has the following choices:

a Move to the residential site.
b Stay in Smith Street and attract his traditional customers back.
c Stay in Smith Street and attract more of the affluent newcomers.

Question

What would you advise?

Wearwell Footwear Ltd

Wearwell Footwear Ltd is a medium sized company with a single factory at Swindon, Wiltshire. The company designs, manufactures and distributes a range of footwear, including shoes for persons of all ages, a range of boots, specialised industrial footwear and, in recent years, has been particularly successful in supplying individually-designed footwear for handicapped persons.

The company sells to retail organisations and two mail-order companies. Some orders are received direct from the public for the more specialised types of footwear, as well as from certain hospital management committees. The retail organisations and mail-order companies each have a credit limit of two months, while hospital management committees are limited to three months. Orders from the public are usually formally accepted only on receipt of cash, though a few customers of long standing are granted a period of credit.

The present organisation of the company is illustrated on the chart in Fig 11. In addition, by way of diversification, Wearwell has recently concluded negotiations to acquire a small company, Facilitron Ltd, situated at Fareham in Hampshire, which specialises in general equipment for handicapped persons. The company is long-established with a team of specialist engineers, and with a high proportion of its supervisory and operative personnel having had long service with the company.

Within the transport, office and dispatch unit of Wearwell there is a team of 28 office and dispatch staff and 14 drivers. Jim Langley has recently been made senior supervisor of the transport, office and dispatch staff and reports directly to the production manager. Aged 28, he joined the company only three years ago following experience since leaving school at 16 in retailing (including stores work) and as an insurance representative. Since joining the company as a dispatch clerk he has proved himself to be hardworking and able and his efforts have been rewarded with rapid promotion. Most of the staff in the unit are older than Jim Langley, and several have been with the company for many years. Jim has three assisting supervisors (transport, office, dispatch). Two of them have been passed over for promotion during the past year on vacancies arising within the company, including the position that Jim now holds. The company operates an appraisal system and, as senior supervisor, Jim Langley will be required to make six-monthly reports to the production

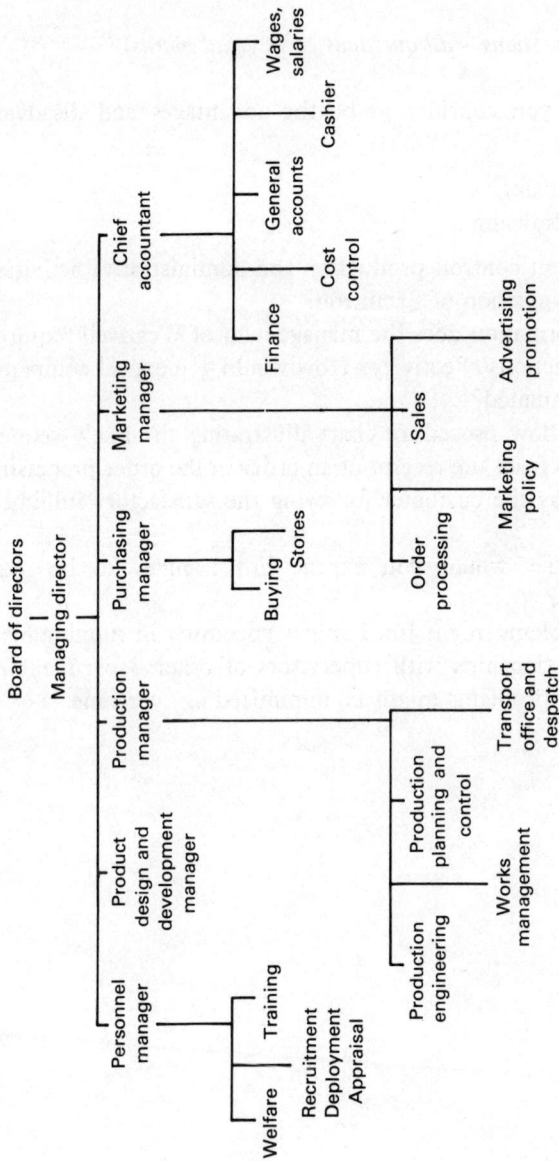

Fig 11 Wearwell Footwear Ltd organisation chart

Chart structure:

Board of directors
Managing director

- Personnel manager
  - Welfare
  - Training
  - Recruitment
  - Deployment
  - Appraisal
- Product design and development manager
- Production manager
  - Production engineering
  - Production planning and control
  - Works management
  - Transport office and despatch
- Purchasing manager
  - Buying
  - Stores
- Marketing manager
  - Order processing
  - Marketing policy
  - Sales
  - Advertising promotion
- Chief accountant
  - Finance
  - Cost control
  - General accounts
  - Cashier
  - Wages, salaries

manager on the performance, the need for training and suitability for promotion of his subordinates.

Questions

(Answer all questions – all questions carry equal marks)

1 What do you consider to be the advantages and disadvantages of Wearwell

- centralising
- decentralising

management control, production and administrative activities following the acquisition of Facilitron?

2 What information does the management of Wearwell require to carry out its functions effectively? How would you expect company policies to be formulated?

3 Design a flow procedure chart illustrating the likely sequence(s) of operations from the receipt of an order in the order processing unit to payment by the customer following the satisfactory fulfilment of the order.

4a What duties would you expect Jim Langley to be required to undertake?

b What problems might Jim Langley encounter in running his unit and in his relationships with supervisors of other departments? Suggest how these problems might be minimised or overcome.

Westborough Bus Company

You have just been appointed to the post of manager of the Westborough Bus Company.

The function of the company is to provide transport to the people of Westborough and its expanding new housing and industrial development. National Bus Services provide transport between Westborough and nearby towns and villages. In the next two years both companies are to use a new bus station which is being built by the local authority as part of an indoor retail trading centre. For this the company will have to pay a rent, yet to be negotiated, for each departure. The main street, now used for picking up passengers, is to be closed to through traffic and buses.

The situation is unusual in that the present manager, due to retire in three months' time, shows every sign of holding his post firmly to the end. He states that as he *has* to retire, *against* his wishes, he will not relinquish any part of his job as manager. His only instructions to you are that it will take that time for you to become acquainted with the organisation.

Though in awe of the current manager, the company's Board members are aware of his weaknesses and glad to be introducing a strong new management. The TV news estimates that it is able to report a major situation of industrial unrest, or even strike action, in the bus company two or three times each year. A result of these frequent disruptions has been that union demands, whether justifiable or not, have been accepted. As a result a number of recently made agreements will have to be negotiated out. Previously, office workers showing independence of thought or potential leadership were promptly repressed but they may have stayed in the company hoping for opportunities to arise.

Orders for capital equipment in the form of buses have gone out of phase and it seems likely that half the stock of 80 buses is due for replacement; this will be your responsibility. The topic is always deferred at Board meetings and has not therefore been discussed for some time. (Buses cost £48 000 each, have a 15-year life and require a major body overhaul and repaint at six- to seven-year intervals. Vehicle life may be extended, at a cost, up to 21 years).

The company is divided into three main functions: traffic, which organises timetables and routes, and this has been your previous speciality; accounts and administration, of which you have a certain amount of knowledge; and engineering of which your knowledge is virtually nil. It will be necessary to nominate people to take charge of these functions. No promotion possibilities are available in engineering.

There is an operating staff of 150 driver/conductors, 16 inspectors and 60 workshop staff. The clerical and administrative staff number 35, including yourself.

The national economy should be assumed to be operating in conditions of reasonable prosperity with 10 per cent inflation.

In answering the questions you are required to:

a   Make clear any reasonable assumptions you feel are necessary.
b   Make clear any national circumstances if you are not basing your answer in the context of the UK.

Questions

1   Set out your work programme for the *next* three months. Use the following headings:

    a   Relationship with current manager.
    b   Relationship with management committee.
    c   Organisation structure and recruitment of managers.
    d   Updating of vehicle fleet.
    e   Personnel.
    f   Relationship with trade unions.
    g   Bus services.   *(80 marks)*

2   Indicate how you would proceed in the *first* three months of taking over control from the retiring manager.   *(20 marks)*

Menlath Products

Menlath Products is an international company concerned with food preservation and distribution. Its mode of operation is to establish plants in primary production areas to can or freeze fruits or fish (and sometimes meat) and distribute these products, mostly through European outlets under various brand names. Where local conditions make the operation of subsidiary plants unduly difficult (eg because of local laws), it enters into long term contracts with local operators. Menlath provides a managerial and technical advisory service in these circumstances and maintains quality standards vigorously.

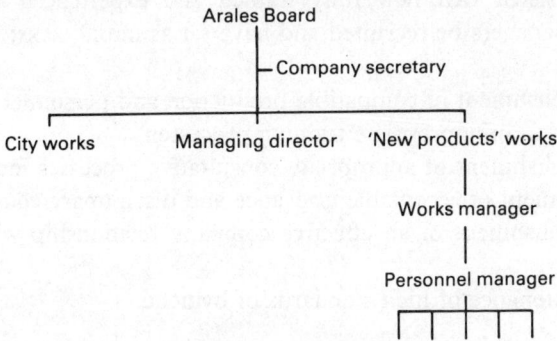

Fig 12 Arales Foods organisation chart

Arales Foods (Fig 12) is a company which has recently entered into a large contract with Menlath for the provision of local grown, or imported (from neighbouring countries) tropical and semi-tropical fruits, vegetables and sauces. Arales Foods, with the help of government and international grants, has established a new processing plant some 12 kilometres from the capital's centre but with ready access to roads, docks and a railway travelling to the country's interior. Labour will necessarily have to be recruited and since public transport is inadequate the company will have to provide transport. Supervisors may come from an older processing plant in the city. It is thought that the labour requirements will be for:
5 supervisors
45 full-time process workers
15 labourers, cleaners, etc

and between 20 and 80 part-time workers dependent upon seasonal factors. Additional full-time workers may also be required at seasonal or contractual peaks.

Menlath Products is insistent that:

a   good welfare facilities are to be given to staff.
b   very high standards of hygiene are maintained.
c   quality control is very strict.

Arales's present managerial practices are simple in its old factory. The production line is organised on a conveyor belt principle giving very little chance of social interaction. The current recruitment of staff is based upon a casual interview by supervisors who select their own teams. Training, on a formal basis, is non-existent. Staff turnover has been at 50 per cent and the plant lacks any feeling of friendliness.

Menlath management has entered into the arrangement with Arales with some misgivings but has been impressed by Arales management's capacity to 'deliver the goods' on existing short term contracts. Menlath has now insisted that new fully trained and experienced works and personnel managers be recruited and have set as initial tasks:

a   the establishment of compatible production and personnel policies.
b   the creation of appropriate training processes.
c   the establishment of appropriate consultative processes including the establishment of acceptable grievance and disciplinary codes.
d   the establishment of an effective company relationship with its employees.
e   the maintenance of high standards of hygiene.

Question

Assume that you have been appointed to one of the new posts. Give your views and intentions relating to the points noted above in the form of a report to Arales Board bearing in mind the need to justify an approach which though meeting Menlath's requirements will be alien to Arales Board.

Victoria Printing Co Ltd

For some time the managing director of Victoria Printing had been concerned about the differing administration systems which were in operation throughout the company. He believed that they were not operating as effectively as required, and was concerned about the effect that this could be having on communication and company efficiency.

Before the monthly Board meeting in March 1983, he discussed his concern with senior managers in the company and it was agreed to employ a consultant to undertake an appraisal of company administration. It was hoped the survey would lead to recommendations designed to strengthen coordination, reduce costs and increase efficiency. Since it had an interface with all other departments in the company as well as with the firm's customers, management including Mr Rupert Green, the sales manager, agreed that the sales administration office would make an ideal starting point for the survey.

The organisation of the sales administration office

The sales administration office at Victoria Printing was the responsibility of Mr Tom Cook, sales office supervisor, and he reported directly to Mr Green. The work of the department consisted of receiving orders from customers in writing or verbally over the telephone, processing these orders, preparing and issuing works orders, typing and issuing sales invoices and entering stock records, sales representatives' correspondence and reports, and general correspondence and filing associated with the office routine.

The organisation of the office, which had an open plan layout, was not clearly defined and the general atmosphere was informal. Individual activities were not clearly delineated, as all employees except typists were designated sales administrators, and staff could be observed carrying out several different tasks during the course of the day. For instance, although the office employed only three typists, as many as five people could sometimes be observed typing invoices, orders and general correspondence. Similarly, on warehouse stock records, which required two people full-time, it was possible to observe four or five people helping to clear up any backlog of bookings.

As office supervisor, Mr Cook controlled the work of 12 staff, four men and eight women, and his style of management contributed considerably to the relaxed, if apparently sometimes undirected, pace of life in the department. Little official overtime was recorded although staff could regularly be observed working after the company stopping time of 5.00 pm. This was due to Tom Cook's belief that a flexible approach to the supervision of working hours invoked a sense of responsibility in staff and improved motivation. Consequently, the office was rarely fully staffed at 8.30 am when the day commenced, much to the annoyance of other managers in the company who adhered strictly to the official working day. However, most managers in the company agreed that the department operated satisfactorily and some openly envied the working relationship which Tom Cook had established in his department.

The consultant's survey

One week after the senior managers' meeting, Mr Green called Tom Cook into his office and outlined the background to the decision to employ a consultant. He explained the reasons for the survey and confirmed that the consultant, Mr Gerald Cross, would arrive the next day and would be starting his work in the sales administration office.

When Mr Cross arrived at 9.00 am the following day, he spent the first two hours in Mr Green's office, talking to the sales manager. Mr Green introduced the consultant to Tom Cook and they spent most of the next week together analysing various routines, discussing the activities which were carried out in the office, and the specific function of each member of staff. During this time, Mr Cross made copious notes and also spent some time talking to each staff member at their office desk. As the week progressed, Mr Cook discovered that he was having increasing difficulty in being specific about many things, including his own role in the department. For example, he did not believe that he adequately justified the job rotation which occurred, and he found it difficult to evaluate the benefits of his flexible approach to time keeping and individual responsibility. However, at the end of the period Mr Cross appeared to be extremely satisfied with their discussions, and told Mr Cook he would be returning after he had studied the information he had gathered and completed his survey throughout the company.

During the months from April to June 1983, Tom Cook occasionally saw Mr Cross at work in other offices in the company, but he did not have any opportunity for a detailed talk with the consultant. However, in July 1983, just before Victoria Printing Co Ltd was due to close down for the annual summer holiday, Tom Cook was again called to Mr Green's office, where the sales manager and Mr Cross outlined plans for the reorganisation of the sales administration office. Job descriptions were to be prepared for each individual, including Tom Cook and Mr Green, and clerical work measurement was to be carried out on the repetitive element of work in the office. Mr Cross estimated that this was about 60 per cent of all the activities in the office. Work flow was to be further analysed to examine the possibility of a revised layout for the office and the warehouse stock records were to be mechanised and transferred to the warehouse to avoid the problem of duplication. Finally, the production planners, numbering six in total, would be transferred to Mr Cook's control. It was proposed that they should each pair up with a sales administrator to make a team of two people who would be responsible for a particular part of the company's product range, from receipt of orders to dispatch of goods.

When he left the sales manager's office, Mr Cook was seriously concerned about the new proposals, which he felt had been designed from the beginning to reorganise his office. He believed that the team concept would be a difficult one to apply and that it called for a management style different from his own.

Questions

1 Analyse the case and comment upon the manner in which the appraisal of the organisation and administration was undertaken. What do you think were the good points and what was unproductive?
2 Compare and contrast Tom Cook's approach to supervising the sales administration office with the changes proposed by the consultant. What are the significant differences and what factors affect the situation?
3 As Tom Cook, how would you introduce the proposed changes to your staff and how would you deal with any misgivings that might be expressed.
4 The majority of the sales administration staff are members of a 'white collar' union. What are the implications for future industrial relations of the action which management has taken so far?
5 State why you believe Tom Cook is, or is not, the right man to head the reorganised office.
6 Tom Cook consults you about the proposed changes in the company. How would you convince him that he should accept the changes?

A matter of choice

Driving to the office on the morning of his 49th birthday, Brian Carton thought, as he had done so often before in the last 10 years, that perhaps it was time for a change. Although apprenticed in the furniture trade, Brian had seen while in his twenties that a marketing career offered greater satisfaction and considerably better material rewards than the work for which he was first trained. He had therefore switched careers and now worked as a marketing executive for a large international conglomerate with interests in many markets but particular strengths in several aspects of communications including TV programme-making, publishing and computer-based information systems. Brian's particular concern was the marketing of a range of special interest technical and scientific magazines in the UK and overseas.

Carton enjoyed his work and had been with his present employer for some 15 years, advancing gradually in his marketing career, particularly after successfully completing a part-time course of study leading to the Institute of Marketing's Diploma. Nevertheless he had retained his interest in craft work and had built up a modest spare-time business restoring antique furniture. He had an established circle of private clients and also undertook some work under contract from local antique dealers. His prices were competitive and, because he had been properly apprenticed, the quality of his work was first class. As a consequence, he was always being offered more work than he could handle on a part-time basis and he had had to form a small limited company with his wife and son as co-directors to ensure that matters such as VAT were properly handled. To make the considerable amount of time he spent on this sideline more immediately profitable to him, Brian had recently invested several hundred pounds in secondhand woodworking machinery, which he had installed in the garage-cum-workshop of his home. The resulting increase in productivity gave him the opportunity to begin to make, largely for his own personal satisfaction, very small quantities of top quality reproduction Victorian and Edwardian furniture for which he found a ready market. In the light of this success his wife had suggested that he design kits for some of the simpler pieces of furniture and market them to amateur woodworkers for them to finish and assemble themselves. The investment in stock and promotion would not be large and his professional marketing experience enabled him to pinpoint precisely how and where the most cost-effective promotion of the kits could be directed. Successful development of the idea could give Brian the chance to run his own business full-time.

But this was not the only opportunity Carton was reviewing. Much of his marketing expertise was directed towards securing annual subscriptions for the specialist magazines with which he was concerned. He knew that the distribution problems faced by any minority interest publication would be overcome if readers placed orders direct with the publisher in advance. But there was considerable consumer resistance to buying subscriptions, at least in the home market, and there existed no satisfactory means of marketing or promoting them. However, he had recently hit upon the idea of launching magazine subscription tokens, on the analogy of book tokens. He was sure that if a magazine token could be made available which allowed people to exchange it for one or more of a wide range of popular and specialist titles it would have considerable consumer appeal, particularly to people looking for presents for men.

The snag seemed to be that potential customers for magazine tokens would probably be concentrated in the large multiple newsagents but the newsagents themselves would be unlikely to be interested in selling the tokens because each one they sold could lose them magazine sales. The magazine publishers might also be wary about joining a scheme which was disliked by the 'trade'.

Whether or not that assessment was correct, Brian knew that to launch such a scheme he would have to resign from his job, with all the risk but potential reward that entailed. Fortunately, he no longer had family commitments so the option was tempting. Also, he had already been offered the necessary investment backing he would need.

Questions

1 Advise Brian Carton on the course of action he should take.
2 What needs to be done to turn the magazine token idea into a marketable product?
3 Make detailed recommendations for the promotion of:
   - the furniture kits
   - the magazine tokens

Jamesons Ltd

Jamesons Ltd is a national chain of supermarkets carrying food, drink and household goods. A new branch superstore which will be the company's largest in the country has been built close to a large provincial city.

The appointment policy of the company for departmental managers is that of promotion from within the company; a general manager for the store has already been appointed. He was previously general manager of a smaller branch. A shortlist of three candidates has been drawn up for the post of manager of the clerical services department; the person appointed will in turn appoint members of the department.

The new store is being equipped with modern electronic technology for use in all departments, including stock control and ordering, accounts, personnel and clerical services.

- John Lynne, currently head of the clerical services department in a smaller established branch, is 47 and has been with the company since leaving school. He has few formal qualifications and no training in, or experience of, electronic business technology. He is, however, an efficient supervisor, well respected and popular with all members of his present department.

- Joanne Abbot (40), since joining the company 10 years ago, has taken considerable trouble to familiarise herself with new developments in office technology. She is ambitious and extremely efficient but her experience is limited to supervising a fairly small department.

- Thomas Benjamin (30), a Business Studies graduate, has been with the company for four years and has shown flair and enthusiasm in helping to organise a computer-based clerical services department in one of the larger branches in the company. His manner is cool, can tend to impatience and, though he is respected by members of his present department, he tends unwittingly to antagonise members of other departments.

The three candidates are to be interviewed for the new post. Individual appraisal discussions have already taken place. Each candidate has been asked to prepare for the formal interviews a presentation of his/her own outline proposals for the structure and organisation of the new department.

Questions

1 Outline the main features which would be required in a training programme, to be introduced by the successful candidate, designed to ensure that each member of the department is appropriately prepared to work effectively with the new technology to be used.

2 Each candidate if appointed would experience different problems of leadership.

   a Identify the major problems of supervisory leadership.

   b Suggest particular remedies that each candidate might adopt.

3 a Describe the advantages of holding individual staff appraisal interviews prior to the selection interviews in this case.

   b Suggest some reasons for asking candidates to prepare presentations of outline proposals for the new department.

4 Explain the main features of current legislation relating to employment (engagements and dismissals), with which the successful candidate will be concerned in organising the new department.

Powa Drill Co Ltd

The Powa Drill Co Ltd was originally founded in 1955 as a partnership between Charles Boxgrove, an ex-World War II army officer in the Royal Engineers, and Keith Mitchelson, a distributor of government surplus electrical equipment.

The partnership was started on a 'shoe-string' in prefabricated buildings adjoining Keith Mitchelson's Army Surplus Store in Uxbridge Road, Stone. In a post-war period of rapid expansion, the partnership prospered and was formed into a limited company in 1961. By 1968, the company had an annual turnover of £860 000, mainly in the commercial drill market of the construction industry. Powa Drill's hand-held drills were sold through a network of retail ironmongers over their trade sales counters.

In 1970, Keith Mitchelson died suddenly and, with the help of a bank loan, Charles Boxgrove was able to secure a majority shareholding in the company and the post of chairman of the Board and managing director. At about this time, a local industrialist, Sir Harold Wentworth, bought shares in the firm and secured for Powa Drill the lease on a factory on the Stone Industrial Estate, since the company was in urgent need of additional space.

With Sir Harold's support, the company developed a plan in the early 1970s to penetrate the expanding market for DIY home users of electric drills. Thus a design team was established, and a successful new product launched on 1 May 1973 called the 'Home-maka Powadrill'. As a result of the innovative design of its gearing mechanism, the drill proved extremely versatile and sales quickly climbed.

To meet demand, a second factory was leased in 1974 on the Ritchfield Industrial Estate, Brading, and production was rationalised, with the commercial market range of drills being manufactured in Stone, and the DIY range in Brading. At this time, the company moved into a new head office building in Marlton equidistant from both factories.

In 1974, the first effects of the recession in the construction industry were felt, and Powa Drill found itself short of finance with which to redevelop and redirect its product range. Fortunately, a wealthy widow stepped into the breach. In her sixties, Mrs Harriet Finch-Barton was the widow of a retired merchant banker who had left her with a considerable amount of disposable assets. Partly due to Charles Boxgrove's powers of persuasion, Mrs Finch-Barton invested a considerable sum in Powa Drill and was appointed to its Board of directors. She also proved a most valuable human asset, since it was she who persuaded the Board to diversify into labour-saving, electricity-powered garden tools – such as grass-cutters, strimmers, hedge-trimmers and rotavators.

At about this time, progress was being made at the Brading factory in developing a range of accessories built around the heavy-duty Home-maka drill which would enable a wider range of functions to be performed including cutting timber, sanding, and effecting mitre joints. By March 1984, the Research and Development staff were on the brink of bringing to a successful conclusion the prototype testing of a comprehensive kit, including a metal bench, which would handle almost any job around the house in carpentry and general maintenance terms. The kit was scheduled to retail at around £150.

Currently, the company's structure is as shown below (see also Fig 13 page 120):

Locations	*Head office*:
	Powa Drill House, Cookham Road, Marlton
	Commercial and garden tool factory:
	London Road Industrial Estate, Stone
	Home and DIY factory:
	Ritchfield Industrial Estate, Brading

Employees	Head office:	51
	Stone factory:	135
	Brading factory:	162

Current product range	Konstrukta Commercial Drills
	Home-maka DIY Drills
	Grass Cutta Mowers
	Trimmit Hedge Trimmers
	Diggit Rotavators
	Home-builda Home Maintenance Kit

Annual turnover	Commercial drills:	£1.4 million
	DIY drills/kits:	£2.7 million
	Garden equipment:	£1.1 million
	Total:	£5.2 million

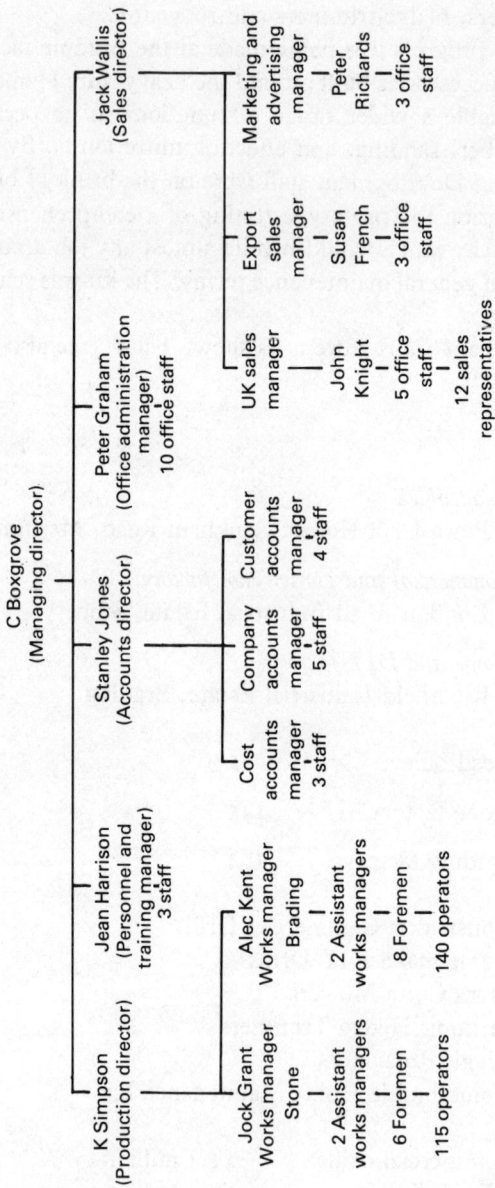

Fig 13 Powa Drill Co Ltd organisation chart

In addition, there was Gordon Dixon and a team of three who ran the company's transport department, and who were responsible for some 15 vehicles, comprising lorries and vans.

Company organisation	Board of directors:
	Charles Boxgrove, chairman and
	managing director
	Sir Harold Wentworth
	Mrs Harriet Finch-Barton
	Mr Stanley Jones, accounts director
	Mr Kenneth Simpson, production director
	Mr Jack Wallis, sales director

Since the late 1960s, the company's efforts have been concentrated upon production, marketing and selling. Thus the acquisition of office equipment and information processing systems evolved somewhat haphazardly, as each department perceived a particular need. Moreover, the office administration department was only created in an effectively functioning form in 1979, and there was still a great deal to be achieved in formulating a coherent information processing policy.

The head office functions on a PABX telephone switchboard system and the receptionist operates the telex machine. In addition, there is a Rank Xerox photocopier for interdepartmental use, together with a conventional mailroom. There are some 24 internal telephone extensions with a total of 10 outside lines. The departmental office equipment such as typewriters, etc is on average six years old.

Recent Board of directors meeting

Item 6 on the agenda is: Updating of communications system and future policy.

Mrs Harriet Finch-Barton addresses the Board:

'I must tell you about my recent visit to the Information Technology Exhibition at the Barbican! It was a revelation, I don't mind telling you! We've got to accept the fact that, in information processing terms, we're still operating in the Dark Ages – what we need is a long hard look at the nature and scope of our current equipment and to move into a comprehensive word and data processing system. I was talking to one of the exhibitors who reckons that it's quite possible to process five times the information with about half the staff! And the information is readily accessible to help the board in making effective decisions. . . .'

Sir Harold Wentworth:

'I'm not so sure about the position with regard to trimming back on admin staff, but I think Harriet is right in principle. According to the last set of management accounts figures, we should have a not inconsiderable sum to invest in this sort of rationalising project.'

Stanley Jones, accounts director:

'Well, I don't need to remind you about the inadequacy of the Jaybees Computer – its replacement has been long overdue, and the current software packages in accounting terms could save a lot of time, as well as providing more up-to-date information. I think it's high time we moved on this one. . . .'

With little more discussion, other than general supportive remarks about the need to move into the 1980s promptly, the Board voted to install a suitable system as soon as possible.

Overheard in the head office ladies cloakroom:

'. . . Well, I suppose we might as well start looking for another position. By all accounts, half of us in office admin will be made redundant when this new all singing, all dancing word processor watchamicallit is set up!'

'I heard they're ever so bad for your eyes – imagine looking at a flickering green screen all day long!'

'And they reckon they can keep a check on how much you've typed in an hour!'

'No!'

'Yes! Take it from me, the best days are already over here!'

Peter Richards to Sue French:

'You going to this demo of the proposed computer system tomorrow?'

'What new system?'

'The one Stanley Jones has arranged in accounts.'

'Be nice to know it was happening. What time is it?'

'I'm not sure – anyway, it's probably only good for number-crunching if I know Stan!'

Senior shop steward at Brading factory, addressing monthly union meeting:

Machine operator:

'What about this computer set-up they're all talking about. I reckon it'll be used to jack up our piece work rates if we're not careful. I've heard tell management's gonna use it to analyse productivity from top to bottom!'

Senior shop steward: (embarrassed)

'Don't you worry Sam, we'll not let 'em steal a march on this one – in fact, I've got it on the agenda for the next Works Committee meeting.'

Voice from back:

'And about time too!'

Jean Harrison to John Knight:

'Confidentially, John, I think this whole computerisation thing is going to rebound on us if we're not careful – the whole place is rife with rumour and counter rumour. Surely there's a better way of going over to a more fully computerised set-up than putting on a series of demonstrations without much prior notice or explanatory follow-up!'

Questions

1 How should the Board of directors, in your opinion, set about the acquisition and installation of a suitable computerised information system?
2 What are the needs in interpersonal terms and for internal communications which are highlighted by the case study when such an acquisition is being considered?
3 Can you suggest any restructuring of the company which might be undertaken as part of the installation/implementation of introducing an extensive computerised information processing system?

'New Industrial Products' (MW) Ltd (NIP) – II

'NIP' was formed in 1960 to manufacture road signs to meet the expected and actual demand deriving from the expansion of the motorways and the general road programme.

The manufacturing processes included metal fabrication, sheet metal work, paintshop and fairly simple electrical work, complex electrical work and plastic extrusion work being subcontracted.

The company was originally highly successful and collected a labour force attracted by the opportunity of high earnings and fairly pleasant working conditions. The factory is situated on an industrial estate and although the firm is a subsidiary of a major multi-industry concern, it has been left largely to its own devices.

The growth of the labour force (now 200) has brought with it a rapid awareness of the advantages of trade union membership as a result of which the company joined the Employee's Association two years ago. The company organisation chart is shown in Fig 14 and the personalities are detailed below. Rowbotham is a junior director of the parent company.

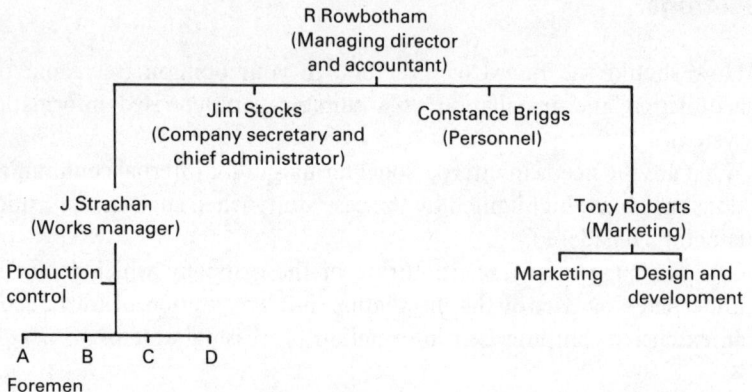

Fig 14 NIP organisation chart

Managing director

Robert Rowbotham is now 54 years old and became the managing director nine years ago following six years as finance director in another company.

He is recognised as a very able managing director who believes that management must operate with the minimum of formality and the maximum of participation in decision making. He encourages the use of Christian names and discourages the development of status symbols. At the same time, he is a fanatic for efficiency from others as well as himself and most employees regard him as an exhausting person to work with.

Works manager

John Strachan is 49 years of age and was appointed to his present position 11 years ago having been works manager of a coach building company. He is accepted by all concerned as a capable manager. He considers that his chief contribution to the firm's success has been the improved production methods and closer control made possible by the efficient work study department he has built up from scratch. He has recently been much concerned with quality control procedures.

Marketing manager

Tony Roberts, 34 years old, has just joined the company having been the merchandise manager of one of the country's largest supermarkets. He has accepted a drop in salary but sees special opportunities as the company enters new markets.

Company secretary

Jim Stocks is now 58 years old, joined the company at the beginning as secretary. Though a company secretary and a very able administrator who performs the technical aspects of his tasks efficiently and effectively, he is a poor leader. He is short-tempered with subordinates, has very little patience and is, as a result, both feared and disliked in the office. He has announced his intention of retiring in six months' time.

Personnel manager

Constance Briggs, aged 37 years, has been in her present job for five years. She was an assistant personnel manager in a sister company for five years. She was appointed to personnel because the managing director is of the opinion that a woman should be introduced into the management team, since half the labour force is female. She has been a success so far, though her lack of knowledge of production technology caused trouble with the works manager for the first few months. This has now been settled – the managing director made it clear that she 'was his man'. She is seeking an appointment with a larger company so that she can further her career.

Labour relations

Labour relations were good until 1981 when some strain was felt due to short-time work and the dismissal of two maintenance men for 'incompetence'. Additionally, shop floor suspicions that some of the paint being used had toxic potentialities was confirmed and although the material is no longer used the suspicion remains that management is insufficiently concerned with health hazards.

The fact that export orders have kept employment steady has not compensated some of the workers for the fact that different standards have to be met and, on the administration side, the complexities of export procedures have to be mastered.

Last year the company decided to enter the shopfitting business, particularly in the provision of shelving, signs and other plasticised material with particular reference to the equipping of hypermarkets. An initial grant worth £250 000 was secured last year and so far contracts for £800 000 have been secured this year. The change of emphasis in production has put a strain on the design department and new equipment has had to be purchased, not all of which has been integrated smoothly into production lines. The contracts have required intensive work to meet very specific delivery dates and although generous overtime rates have been paid and a productivity bonus (of about 20 per cent) negotiated, there is at present considerable labour stress.

The managing director and the personnel manager have given much thought to employee relations in general and industrial relations in particular. They are well aware of impending changes in employee relations due to, for example, increased trade union membership within the company and recent legislation. They now wish to establish personnel policies to meet the new situation. The work force has already indicated to management its unwillingness to continue to work at current production levels on a 5 per cent wage increase basis.

Questions

(*All questions carry equal marks.*)

1 Suggest a personnel policy appropriate to the company now and state how it could be put into effect. What wages policy would you propose?

2 The personnel manager is not satisfied with the company's health and safety policy which was drawn up and issued to all employees under the Health and Safety at Work Act 1974. It is now necessary to take account of more recent legislation and the fact that many employees work away from base on the installation of equipment in customers' premises.

a Devise a health and safety policy you consider to be suitable for NIP (MW) Ltd.

b How do you think the company management ought to handle the matter of safety representatives and safety committees? Give your reasons.

3 The managing director is anxious to improve relationships between the design department, production control, shop floor supervision and the company's clients. What would you propose?

4 What advice would you give the managing director who is concerned about:

a the replacement of the company secretary?

b the integration of the new marketing manager within the management team?

c the probable departure of Constance Briggs?

5 What has sociology and psychology to suggest about the way in which the management team can best operate and how it can face the difficulties deriving from the present industrial climate?

Bek Brothers

Bek Brothers is a major department store in the centre of Ferningbridge. It is a private limited company with an annual turnover of £5 million. There is no street parking but there is a large municipal car park 300 yards away from the store. There are three other department stores in the city. Two belong to nationally owned chain companies with an effective promotion and aggressive pricing policy.

The store was established in 1870 and its structure and layout is antiquated. The owners are members of the family and believe in a traditional approach to retailing.

There are five storeys with the top one being devoted entirely to administration. The other floors are divided into the following 14 departments:

Menswear	Food
Ladies fashions	Bedding/linens
Shoe department	Furniture/carpets
Childrenswear	Electrical goods
Toys	Soft furnishings
Hardware	Kitchenware
Perfumery	Fancy goods/gift department

The range of merchandise is wide because of the traditional approach adopted by the owners.

The extent of personal service is high, not only in terms of the selling departments but other facilities offered to the customers. Many of these services are costly to operate, for example the alterations workshop.

Trading problems are increasing. The firm has received a detailed report indicating likely future trends in the distributive industry. Many of the implications of the report are directly relevant to the firm in its local market. Existing competition is becoming increasingly aggressive. The other department stores have adopted a more effective trading policy involving rationalisation and pricing and their share of the market is increasing for Bek Brothers' merchandise. The situation is now particularly critical since the establishment of an off-centre superstore which is rapidly gaining a reputation for good quality and highly competitive merchandise, particularly in food and household goods.

It is essential for the survival of Bek Brothers that a rationalisation programme be introduced to maintain existing turnover in response to market developments. New methods and techniques in distribution need also to be considered. There are a number of other critical problems to be analysed.

A high proportion of turnover is sales to foreign tourists. Much of the merchandise is imported.

The present government is committed to strict monetary and fiscal policies involving high interest rates, a tight money supply and cuts in the public sector borrowing rate.

Questions

1 What will be the effects of the government's economic policies on Bek Brothers?

2a Describe the methods Bek Brothers can employ to price its products.

 b What must the company take into account when pricing its products?

3a Identify the main elements of a rationalisation programme.

 b What information does the firm require in order to undertake this programme? What will be the sources of information and how will this information be used by the company?

4a Comment on the usefulness of externally published research in this context.

 b Comment on likely future market developments for Bek Brothers.

5 What balance is required in the level of personal service and the range of services offered by Bek Brothers in response to likely trends?

6a What will be the effects of a rationalisation programme on staffing levels?

 b What methods of communication could the firm employ to inform employees of any changes made?

 c What would be the legal responsibility of the firm and the role of a trade union in this situation?

7 Outline the main duties imposed on employers and employees of Bek Brothers by the Health and Safety at Work Act 1974.

8 Devise an acceptable disciplinary/grievance procedure that will comply with regulations and have acceptability to unions. Include examples that would be covered by your suggestions and indicate which of your disciplinary procedures would apply to each. Clearly indicate positions of responsibility within the procedure.

Strathclyde Holdings Ltd*

Company background

Strathclyde Holdings Ltd is a holding company for a group of subsidiaries involved in a wide range of activities in building and construction, property development, shopfitting and interior decoration. It has grown rapidly in the past 20 years through acquisition and is now a publicly quoted company. Its sales turnover for 1982/83 was £104 million, profits were £5.2 million (90 per cent of which came from two major subsidiaries), and it employs about 12 000 people.

The group was originally formed in 1961 by the amalgamation of several independent companies, three of which had been established for more than 75 years. Since then the company has grown through acquisition and by diversifying into a range of associated areas. These have been grouped into three main divisions: building and construction, property development, and shopfitting and interior decoration.

Each of the subsidiaries has retained a large degree of independence in its operations, and has managed to a greater or lesser extent to preserve its own character. In several of the subsidiaries the original founders of the company, or their relatives, occupy senior management positions.

In recent years, the parent company has attempted to introduce a greater degree of rationalisation and integration between member companies in the group, although this has met with considerable resistance in some subsidiaries. A central services group has been set up to provide assistance for subsidiaries in the areas of finance, personnel, data processing and marketing. A new appointment of group purchasing manager has been established to add to these central services.

Group purchasing activities

The group as a whole bought £54.3 million worth of products or services in 1982/83. However, each subsidiary had virtually complete autonomy in its buying decisions, with no central guidance, policy, training or group negotiation. While there was no suggestion that individual buying units

* The case is based upon a real company and describes a real situation. However, to preserve confidentiality, certain names and data have been disguised.

were not performing effectively, it was felt that such a diversity of buying decisions must inhibit the group in its attempts to use its total buying power effectively.

Therefore, a decision was taken to appoint a group purchasing manager, whose objectives would be to achieve savings of between $\frac{1}{2}$ and 1 per cent on the total costs of raw materials, services, fixtures and fittings and other consumables, and capital items other than major engineering projects. This would be achieved by coordinating the buying activities of various parts of the group, by originating training and guidance for those in purchasing positions, and by examining all purchasing procedures. He would not normally be responsible for individual negotiations.

Group spending* in the year ending June 1983 accounted for 55 per cent of total group costs. For some subsidiaries, purchase cost was a significantly greater component than others, but the percentage of costs accounted for by bought-in items never fell below 35 per cent for any individual subsidiary.

The number and type of items bought in varied considerably between subsidiaries. However, there was no readily available record of the number and volume of items purchased. In a preliminary survey conducted by the group purchasing manager, the majority of buyers spoken to were unable to provide an estimate of the total number of items purchased by them without a substantial amount of extra work. In two subsidiaries with separate purchasing departments such figures were available and a summary analysis indicated that in those subsidiaries 16 per cent of all items purchased had contributed 80 per cent of purchase cost in 1982/83.

The same preliminary survey identified 54 people involved with buying in some form within the group, although an analysis of the number of authorised signatories suggested that this number may have been understated. However, from an analysis of purchase orders placed only 10 people bought or managed the purchase of 74 per cent of the group's spending.

No information was available on the quality of education and training of people involved with purchasing in the group as a whole. However, the group training department reported that in recent years only one course relating to buying had been organised in-house. None of those attending this course held purchasing responsibilities.

With the exception of overhead budgets, only two of the buyers interviewed in the preliminary survey reported holding a quantified budget target or objective relating to their purchasing activities. Even in those areas where a purchase price variance budget existed, it was not considered by the buyer to relate to purchasing cost control performance. There was little or no evidence of the formal measurement of supplier

* Defined as any service, material, component, plant, equipment or utility obtained from outside the group (excluding major capital projects).

delivery and quality performance, and no formal cost reduction or price increase avoidance programmes. None of those interviewed reported working within a framework of formal purchasing policies. No purchasing DP system existed within the group, although the need had been recognised by several subsidiaries.

Finally, little attempt appeared to have been made to use cost escalation budgets as part of a cost reduction or cost avoidance activity. The majority of agreed factors for 1982/83 appeared to have been based on information received from forecasting specialists, trade associations and suppliers, and the resulting budgets therefore reflected the forecast rate of national inflation rather than those which might have been achieved by a programme of cost reduction.

Situation review

Following an initial fact finding review of the purchasing activity within the group, the group purchasing manager sent the following memorandum to the group managing director.

TO: Mr WA Lumsden, group managing director, Strathclyde Holdings Limited.

FROM: Mr JWR Carrigan, group purchasing manager.

PURCHASING

Attached are the results of the previously discussed fact finding review of the group's purchasing activities. You should note that it was my intention during the review to gain a working knowledge of our purchasing without requesting an excessive amount of your staff's time. This resulted in some estimates being used. The report and appendices should therefore be viewed as a basis for discussion rather than a final statement.

Although the information collected, along with general impressions gained from conversations with a variety of personnel involved in purchasing, indicated that many of our buying activities are being performed satisfactorily, I do believe that scope does exist for improvement. Because of the diverse nature of the group, it is not possible to table one set of proposals which would be valid in each area. The extent of our purchasing activities is so wide that even if one approach was feasible, I would not be confident that my understanding, at this stage, of the requirements of all the major buying centres would be sufficient to allow meaningful proposals to be formulated.

I therefore seek your approval for the next phase of the exercise, which would be to hold more detailed discussions with senior members of your staff with a view to agreeing specific actions to improve purchasing performance.

JWRC/CM 20 September 1983

A plan of action

Mr Carrigan presented the findings of his initial report to the main Board in October 1983. The following is an extract from the Minutes.

137 PURCHASING (GB 98/83)
JWR Carrigan wishes to confirm the potential for improvement and to determine what changes are necessary to achieve improvement.

It was agreed that he should discuss with H Greenfield the selection of a production area for investigation and to make specific proposals on organisation, systems, etc.

His report would be available in order to make any agreed changes in time to implement them in the new budget cycle.

Subsequently, JWR Carrigan would propose a timetable for the study of all relevant sections of the rest of the group. No change in job content or organisation will be made in any area until the result of each examination has been discussed with those concerned.

His instructions were explicit. He was to identify a suitable part of the group for study, and make specific proposals for improvements to the purchasing function. Depending on how successful this was, he was then to examine the purchasing activity of the rest of the group. In discussion with members of the group Board, it was agreed that the shopfitting and interior decorating division would be the best place to start this review. The shopfitting and interior decorating division of Strathclyde Holdings was made up of three subsidiary companies. These companies' activities were coordinated more closely than those of the rest of the group, because of their similar activities. Reddington Contracts Ltd was involved in shop installation work and had major contracts with the larger multiples as well as many small independent contracts for conversions or new installations. Barnton Fittings Ltd tended to concentrate on hotel and bar fittings and fixtures with some cafe and restaurant work. Symington Contract and Furnishings Ltd was primarily involved in interior decoration and contract furnishing.

Barnton Fittings Ltd had the greatest identifiable expenditure on bought items, and therefore it was decided that Mr Carrigan should begin his investigations in this company.

Barnton Fittings Ltd – background to the purchasing function

Barnton Fittings Ltd had a sales turnover of £6.4 million in the year ending 30 June 1983. Of this, approximately £3.03 million was spent on 27 major groupings of commodities. Approximately 5000 individual items were bought in total.

Supply points	Approximate usage 1982/83
	£000
Barnet	520
Belfast	155
Bromley	220
Edinburgh	590
Leicester	145
Manchester	230
Middlesbrough	120
Newcastle	480
Solihull	450
Southampton	120
	£3030

Fig 15   Barnton Fittings Ltd – supply points

The existing purchasing function buys for 10 field stores located in branch offices throughout the UK (see Fig 15) and in addition supplies a central store and workshop at head office. In 1982/83 42 per cent of purchases were delivered directly to the depots from the suppliers and 58 per cent from group stores.

The role of purchasing within Barnton Fittings Ltd is oriented towards placing orders, expediting and reacting to *ad hoc* depot requirements. Inventory control is the responsibility of a separate stores controller (Fig 16).

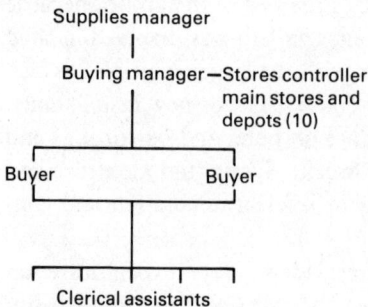

Fig 16   Barnton Fittings Ltd – supplies organisation

Suppliers	£000	Description
B Goodman	544	Coolers
IF Coolers	418	Coolers, meters, fob detectors
Equipment Control	255	Taps, brackets
Pump Equipment	255	Meters, pumpmasters, manifolds
F Stanstead	95	Nylon tubing
Pulman Controls	88	Valves
Gibbon Electronics	85	Cable, circuit breakers, plugs
Tubing Systems	51	Tubing, brass fittings
Alberta Fabrication	44	Draft arms
Wellington Fabrications	34	Cowls
Elliot Manufacturing	34	Cowls
Wilsden Beer Pumps	34	Beer engine couplers
Thorton Beer Machinery	31	Beer engines
Albion Compressors	27	Meters, compressors
Unitech Transformers	20	Transformers
Bilsden Fabricators	17	M Ex cowls
MF Hydraulics	14	Couplers
Ollington Plastics	8	PVC tubing
Control Equipment	5	Valves
Fluid Control	4	Valves, brackets
Burnley Hydraulics	4	'O' rings
	£2.07 million	

Fig 17   Barnton Fittings Ltd – key suppliers (estimated)

Approximately 60 main suppliers are used by the company, of which 21 (35 per cent) contribute 68 per cent of total value (Fig 17). The spend is reasonably stable from year to year, although the degree of significance of individual items changes and each year a number of new items have to be bought for the first time. 42 of the 5000 items bought annually (1 per cent) account for 70 per cent of total expenditure (Fig 18).

A complete and detailed set of specifications does not exist for individual items, although an exercise is under way to rectify the situation. However, the purchasing staff apparently has little influence on specification. In his preliminary investigation, Mr Carrigan found some evidence to suggest that communication frequently took place between Barnton's personnel who were not in the supplies department, and suppliers' representatives. The supplies department was not always informed of the contents of these discussions, which related mainly to engineering matters, such as the need for engineering changes, the introduction of new products, and the evaluation of proposals made by suppliers.

Supplies personnel are also aware that items identical or similar to the ones which they buy are bought elsewhere in the shopfitting and interior decoration division. Some examples include electro-mechanical switches, cable and plugs, nylon and PVC tubing, display material and some machined components. However, they have never had time to investigate this systematically.

A budget for total purchases was established in 1981, and this enabled price variances by period to be calculated for the first time. Purchasing

	By value 1982/83 £000
Sight gauges	3
Avon regulators	4
Fob detectors	14
Compressors	38
CO2 equipment	19
Brass fittings	87
Draft arms	59
Extractors	8
PVC tubing	19
Control units	5
PVC cable	38
Cowls	115
Coolers	1198
Meters	214
Cellar units	182
Drip trays	14
Power units	14
Slave boards	4
Couplers	52
Pressure switches	22
Valves	403
Beer engines	41
Taps and brackets	258
Nylon tubing	122
Cleaning equipment	59
Circuit breakers	32
Transformers	10
	£3.03 million

Analysis by number of items was unavailable, but the supplies manager estimates that approximately 5000 items were purchased across the range of commodities.

Fig 18   Barnton Fittings Ltd – main commodities

performance is measured primarily by comparing actual purchase price variance against budget and actual administration costs with budgeted costs. These figures are reported monthly with an analysis of causes. There is no other system currently used to plan and control the activity of the purchasing function. However, job descriptions do exist for the buying manager and buyer, and are shown in Figs 19 and 20.

a Coordinate the materials and equipment requirements for ten depots and group workshops.

b Consolidate and project future materials and equipment requirements from data supplied.

c Oversee procedures for direct deliveries of equipment from suppliers to depots.

d Assist with the expediting and monitoring of all purchase orders placed with suppliers.

e Oversee and monitor for accuracy all purchasing and stores department documentation, procedures and records.

f Sign purchase orders as an indication of supplies replenishment requirement for authorisation by supplies manager.

g Interview and discuss company requirements with suppliers' representatives.

Fig 19   Barnton Fittings Ltd – regular duties of buying manager

There are no formal purchasing policies, although there are some purchasing procedures, related solely to clerical activities. The lack of adequate computer facilities means that analysis of the existing purchasing a Raise purchase orders for procurement of supplies in accordance with company requirements.

b Issue call-off letters against previously placed bulk purchase orders in accordance with company requirements.

c Oversee and monitor accuracy of purchase record cards.

d Liaise with buying manager and stores controller for effecting direct deliveries to depots.

e Control and carry out the expediting procedures in relation to purchase orders placed with suppliers.

f Carry out effectively and efficiently the procedures laid down for buying and expediting of equipment by the supplies manager.

g Assist the buying manager by ensuring the accurate and effective flow of all supplies department documents, procedures and records.

h Interview and discuss company requirements with suppliers' representatives.

i Supervise and coordinate work flow of five clerical assistants.

Fig 20 Barnton Fittings Ltd – regular duties of buyer

data base has to be done manually. Since these resources have traditionally been limited, the supplies manager has deliberately restricted the amount of planning and reporting of purchasing activities. However, senior management in the company appears to be broadly sympathetic with the need to improve the purchasing function's position in the company.

Questions

All questions carry equal marks

1 If you had been appointed group purchasing manager instead of Mr Carrigan, explain how you would have undertaken your initial fact finding investigation.

(Your explanation should include the main objectives of your investigation, how you would obtain the information you require, and the use you would make of the information. However, your answer need not be restricted to these topics.)

2 In what ways should the role and organisation of the purchasing function in Barnton Fittings Ltd change, if at all? Justify your views. What would be the likely barriers to change?

3 Answer part *a* or *b* but *not both*.

Either

a 'In recent years the parent company has attempted to introduce a greater degree of rationalisation and integration between member companies in the group, although this has met with considerable resistance in some subsidiaries. A central services group has been set up to provide assistance for subsidiaries in the areas of finance, personnel, data processing and marketing. A new appointment of group purchasing manager has been established to add to these central services.'

What major benefits should the company seek from this rational-isation and integration of purchasing?

If you were the group purchasing manager, what actions would you take to achieve these?

Or

b What are the major strategic purchasing problems facing the group purchasing manager?

If you were the group purchasing manager, what actions would you initiate in response to these?

4 Answer part *a* or *b* *not both.*

Either

a The group purchasing manager's objectives included:

'. . . to achieve savings of between $\frac{1}{2}$ and 1 per cent on the total costs of raw materials, services, fixtures and fittings and other consum-ables, and capital items other than major engineering projects.'

With particular reference to Barnton Fittings Ltd, explain how you would seek to achieve such cost reductions.

Or

b 'With the exception of overhead budgets, only two of the buyers interviewed in the preliminary survey reported holding a quantified budget or objective relating to their purchasing activities.'

Prepare proposals for a budgetary planning and control system for purchasing activities throughout the group.

Your proposals should recognise the relationship between the purchasing function and other functions in the group. The proposals are to be presented in a form suitable for consideration by the main Board.

The problem of George Black

When George Black left school at the age of 14 he became an apprentice in the maintenance department of a large steel works. At the outset of his apprenticeship he failed to qualify for a National Certificate course, so at the age of 16 he was diverted into the City and Guilds course. He followed this course with great determination, having been considerably shaken by his early failure. He went to evening classes on three nights a week and after seven years obtained the full Technological Certificate of the City and Guilds. On finishing his apprenticeship, he gained experience by working a 10-inch lathe. During this time his whole attention was directed towards improving his technical qualifications and he became a man extremely skilled in his job, with increasing technical knowledge. He considered technical results more important than anything else.

Black had been with the company for 12 years when a considerable expansion of the works was put in hand. This involved, among other things, the introduction of planned maintenance and the expansion of central maintenance shops by 50 per cent. The company also began to develop a progressive personnel and training policy and the training department regarded Black as being ripe for promotion as soon as a suitable vacancy occurred. So at the age of 26 he was put on a horizontal boring machine, where he worked for five years, being promoted to chargehand and later to shift foreman. He was 31 when appointed day foreman, over the heads of a number of people senior to him.

Now after three years, the position of superintendent has become vacant, for the old superintendent, having frequently been ill, has decided to retire. Black's technical knowledge, high standard of work, his determination to 'get on with the job' and his reliability mark him out as an obvious choice for this vacancy.

Upon appointment, Black is given greater responsibility than a superintendent would normally receive as he had been specially trained by the consultant when the scheme of planned maintenance was introduced. His skill and technical knowledge are universally respected, but *among* his colleagues and subordinates he is regarded as a 'big head'. His experience of coming up the hard way has made him impatient of other people's weaknesses, and he is intolerant of any work which falls short of his own standards. He is constantly chasing his foremen and is rather ruthless in his dealings with them. He works rigidly to planned maintenance procedure, and it is difficult to get him to accept emergency jobs. He treats directives from his superiors merely as a guide on which to base his own decisions, disregarding them entirely on occasion when he feels sure his own decisions are likely to be more effective.

His quick promotion, over the heads of people senior to him, together with his ruthless intolerance, has been causing resentment among the foremen and senior men. In addition, after being a regular attender at branch meetings of the Engineering Union (though he never took more than a general interest in trade union affairs) he has now left the union and this is much resented since his father is a craftsman of long standing who has devoted much of his time to trade union matters and has become secretary to the local Engineering Union branch.

For all those reasons, Black's appointment as superintendent has caused numerous difficulties, particularly since he has been put in control of craftsmen of a different trade from his own, and has to supervise and plan the work of fitters and other maintenance men as well as the machine shop.

It can be said that the new system of promotion instituted in the company, which takes into consideration technical qualifications rather than seniority, has been encountering difficulties because of Black's appointment.

This was brought home rather forcibly to the management by an incident which raised grave doubts as to Black's acceptability, both to his manager and to his colleagues.

The incident concerned the changing of a hoist-motor armature on crane number 005 in the coil storage bay. It was an old crane which was constantly breaking down. The Board of directors had recently decided that it should be replaced with a new one; one of the latest type, with greater lifting capacity. Accordingly, Black had been instructed by his manager to advance this item in the engineering programme and schedule the crane for renewal at an early date.

Black, however, was ahead of the management. He had already planned to have crane 005 modernised within the current replacement programme. In this way the crane would be as efficient as a new one, for a fraction of the cost. With his customary disregard for orders, he had decided to carry on with his own arrangements and was awaiting a favourable opportunity to take the crane out of operation for a thorough inspection. Therefore, when the hoist-motor armature had burned out, he decided to have the crane down for inspection and report at the same time that it was undergoing repairs.

The job was allocated to 'A' gang on the 6 to 2 shift. Black handed to Green, the maintenance shift foreman, detailed instructions in which he had worked out, step by step, the procedures to be followed in the actual doing of the work. Estimated times were assigned to each step, also various items were detailed for inspection and report.

Green thought there was an awful amount of work which was quite unnecessary and which would keep the crane off production longer than was warranted. Black, however, was more concerned with discovering the cause of the repeated failures. He wanted data as a guide to the electrical, mechanical and structural changes needed in his modernisation plan, also he wanted to prevent any further breakdown until the replacement parts were available.

The shift foreman detailed a fitter and his mate, with an electrician, to do the job. These men often boasted, with pride, of the speed with which they could change an armature and get the crane back into production. They, too, thought that much of the work was a waste of time, so that when the production foreman said he wanted the crane in a hurry to avoid a pile-up they were easily persuaded to disregard their own foreman's instructions and make a rush job of it.

Green reported the job as having been completed and it was forgotten, until several days later when the hoist failed again. Black received an urgent request for a speedy repair. He was immediately reminded of the report he had requested from Green and asked to see it. The report made it obvious that his instructions had been disregarded. He was most annoyed and sent word for Green and his fitters to meet him in the coil storage bay where the crane was located. When Black arrived in the coiling bay, Green was already there, talking to Mr White, the production foreman.

Black   Green, what happened to that report I asked for on the condition of this hoist?

Green   I handed it into the office in the usual way.

Black   I've seen that one and it's not what I instructed. How is it you let the men skip the job?

Green   Well, I had something else to do besides watch one fitter and his mate. I started them on the job but while I was away the production people persuaded them to make a quick job of it. They didn't bother with the investigation; they just did what was necessary to get the hoist working – I didn't realise what was happening until I saw the crane in operation again. After that another job cropped up so I let it well alone.

Black   *Well be damned.* The whole purpose of my planned and detailed instructions was to find the cause of the trouble in order to avoid another failure. Now we are back where we started. What's wrong with it this time?

White   What's right with it, you mean. It's always letting us down. About time you scrapped it and installed a new one.

Black   And it's about time you stopped interfering. You stick to production matters, Mr White. And find a driver who can handle a crane. His incompetence and your interference are the cause of this situation. This crane is out of use until I've finished with it. *You*, Green, find out what *is wrong* – and get your men onto it right away. This time stay with them and see that my instructions are followed – to the *letter*.

Green I can't do much now, it's nearly two o'clock. You may as well leave it for the next shift.

Black I said *you* will do it. The next shift are all on scheduled jobs; a bit of overtime may teach you to do as I tell you in future. So get on with it, while I arrange for a mobile auxiliary.

Green Look here Mr Black, I can't work this afternoon. I've made other arrangements. Besides, it isn't fair to the men.

Black Your arrangements do not interest me. I want this job done by *you* and *your* gang – *today*.

With that Black walked away, but when he returned that afternoon neither Green nor his fitters were working and the job had not been touched.

Mr White was very perturbed when he realised that the crane was not being repaired. Work had been piling up and the auxiliary needed plenty of room to move about. He therefore applied for the 'heavy gang' to help clear the gangways. Then, concerned about extra costs and upset by Black's remarks, he reported the incident to his manager.

Questions

1 Identify the problems in this case.
2 Could any have been avoided? If so how?
3 Suggest means of overcoming the immediate difficulties.
4 What can be done to ease tensions and ensure good working relationships in the future?

Square Deal PLC

Square Deal PLC is a newly formed subsidiary company of Square Deal International Inc. The intention is to use it to unify the efforts and improve the profitability of the hitherto separate UK subsidiaries of Arnold PLC, Carlton PLC and Foodrich PLC. At present it has a managing director, an administrative/financial controller and a typist all sharing a large temporary office in central London.

Arnold PLC has 69 food stores, all within a radius of 30 miles from London. Most of them contain either a small restaurant or snack bar and occupy high street or suburban shopping centre locations. It owns one small bakery whose total production supplies 10 stores with bread and cakes. Perishables both for re-sale and restaurant use are bought locally but all other products are bought centrally and distributed from one large warehouse. These products are charged to the stores at selling price on computer printed internal invoices. Store managers are judged solely on revenue. Accounts for each store are produced on the batch computer system at head office which is an old building on the edge of a dockland redevelopment site in East London. The company own the freehold as they do of about half of their food stores.

Carlton PLC has joint managing directors, one in charge of 21 restaurants and one in charge of property development. To date they have built four shopping centres and have plans for three more, all as part of schemes to regenerate old city centres, in the north of England, around 150 miles from London. They lease out the shops with the exception of one per centre which they operate as a restaurant. Both MDs rigidly pursue a 15 per cent annual Return on Investment as their measure of their achievement.

Foodrich PLC was, until last year, a family firm which canned fruit and vegetables from its one factory situated about 100 miles from London, in the west of England. It was bought by Square Deal International Inc with the idea that it would supply 'own label' products to Arnold PLC and large catering packs to both Arnold's and Carlton's restaurants. To do this, Foodrich was obliged to deny supplies to some of their regular customers and re-equip part of its plant to handle the large catering packs. The MD, son of the founder, has worked there for nearly 40 years and runs the company making all decisions, both long term and operational, using his experience and intuition. He is furious to learn that Arnold have not put all their 'own label' business in his direction and Carlton is still buying most catering packs from his competitors while his new plant is grossly underused. Both Arnold's head buyer and the head chef at Carltons claim they get the same quality cheaper from other companies. These recent changes at Foodrich have overwhelmed the MD and one result is that the financial year end accounts up until April will not be ready until some time in August. The accounts are the only defined measure of performance and are usually drawn up by the MD.

The MD of Square Deal PLC has just spent a week touring parts of these three subsidiaries and has returned to the office with a variety of ideas and concerns about ways to unify efforts and improve profitability. To help crystallise some of these ideas he asks the administrator/controller to prepare written statements on various points. Assume you are this administrator/controller.

Questions

1 Discuss the benefits and drawbacks of judging performance on a single criterion such as:

   a revenue, in the case of the store managers.

   b Return on Investment, in the case of Carlton's MDs. *(15 marks)*

2 Explain to what extent Arnold's head buyer and Carlton's head chef are justified in buying catering packs from other companies. *(15 marks)*

3 Explain how MBO could help achieve the desired unification and profit improvements. *(20 marks)*

4 Describe how further computerisation might help in this quest for unification and profit improvement. *(20 marks)*

After you have finished this task, the MD tells you he is toying with the idea of regrouping the company under the name of Square Deal PLC and dividing it into the following divisions, each operating as a profit centre.

Square Deal PLC

Restaurants division	Property division	Food Retail division	Canning division	Bakery division

He is concerned about the effects of such a change on the morale of the managers and other employees so he asks you for a further statement:

5 Discuss ideas that should maintain or improve morale if this regrouping were to take place. *(20 marks)*

6 Highlight any other advantages or difficulties that you foresee in the regrouping idea. *(10 marks)*

Wessex Computers

Wessex Computers has been running for five years now, and it is still virtually a 'one-man business' though there are 20 employees. While the firm sells books, magazines and small 'micro' games, its business is predominantly in microcomputers. Staff thus spend their time in selling computers and persuading clients that package programs are applicable to their business or in providing software packages to suit individual requirements. The employees are nearly all in the 20–25 age group, and very keen and interested in their jobs, obviously involved in learning a trade which has every prospect going for it in the years ahead. Every opportunity is taken to display their wares at computer shows and exhibitions and to help in running courses on micros in an effort to make people aware of the 'user-friendly' nature of the equipment.

The site of the main part of the business is in what was once a main shopping street but has now become bypassed, and is in fact a cul-de-sac. The premises consist of a small shop front with 600 sq ft of shopping area in which are displayed microcomputers, books, computer games, calculators and standard software. Behind is a workroom, and above more workrooms and office space, in all 3000 sq ft. Over the shop itself lived a tenant, who has just left the property so that another 1000 sq ft has become available. The proprietor hopes to use this to solve the storage problems and to create one large room which can be used for setting up a permanent training section. His idea is to charge customers a moderate fee so that their employees can be taught how to run their computers. The staff currently consists of the proprietor, a secretary/bookkeeper, three receptionists/assistants and seven programmers/customer support staff. As this is a small organisation and somewhat overworked the specific tasks are flexible and depend on individual preferences.

The other part of the premises is about five miles away in Embridge; three years ago Wessex Computers had won a local 'Enterprise' competition run by the Corporation, for which the prize was this site rented at a reduced cost. It is used as working quarters for five programmers, two customer support staff involved in repairing and servicing the microcomputers and two administrative staff. Control of these staff and effective charging-out of their work to customers has not proved very satisfactory.

As far as Wessex Computers is concerned, some success has been achieved by lending out the microcomputers free of charge for about ten days or by renting them out at a minimal charge for a month or two so that customers have a chance to get acquainted with them. Ninety per cent of such clients end by buying the machine and to some extent the rental could be offset against the capital cost. The owner is considering going into the leasing business as potential buyers are worried about machines becoming quickly outdated; a financing company deals with the funding of this side of the business. Maintenance work has to be done at times, although most frequently problems are caused by either mishandling of floppy disks by the customers, or failure to read the instruction handbooks carefully. Staff have to spend about one or two hours with each customer teaching them to use the machines even though comprehensive instruction manuals are available.

Some six months ago, with everyone working particularly hard, the record keeping was neglected, and the overdraft increased rapidly. The bank became nervous and was only reassured when an independent accountant was called in to complete the year's accounts, and to produce a report and cash flow forecast for a few months ahead.

Among the accountant's remarks was the comment that the owner was working far too hard, for too many hours, trying to be sales manager, general manager and office manager. Obviously this pressure of work could not be maintained and some aspect of his work had to be shed. Since the least interesting part of the business for him was the 'paper work', and the most interesting was selling microcomputers, meeting people and solving problems with them, he decided to appoint an office manager to take control of office procedures, in the most convenient way.

In dealing with this case study you are required to:

a Make clear any reasonable assumptions you feel are necessary.
b Make clear any national circumstances if you are not basing your answer in the context of the UK.
c Use the following points as a guide towards your answer.

Questions

1 Produce a job specification showing the probable responsibilities of the office manager. (*15 marks*)
2 Prepare a press advertisement covering the vacancy and list other sources which could be used. (*10 marks*)
3 Describe the methods of employment interviewing which could be used. (*20 marks*)
4 Comment briefly on the administrative problems as you see them in this organisation. (*30 marks*)
5 Give a description of the control systems you would install in this business. (*25 marks*)

Appendix

Examination techniques – key verbs

Key verbs often indicate what kind of answer you are expected to give. The following lists those most commonly used in examination questions:

Analyse   examine minutely the constitution

Assess   estimate the value of

Comment   write explanatory notes on

Compare   look for similarities and differences between

Contrast   set in opposition in order to bring out differences

Criticise   give your judgment about the merit of theories or opinions or about the truth of facts, and back your judgment by a discussion of the evidence.

Define   set down the precise meaning of the word or phrase. Show that distinctions implied in the definition are necessary

Describe   give a detailed or graphic account of

Discuss   investigate or examine by argument, sift and debate giving reasons for and against

Evaluate   make an appraisal of the worth of something, in the light of its truth and utility; include to a lesser degree, your personal opinion

Explain   to make plain, to interpret, and to account for

Illustrate   use a figure or diagram to explain or clarify, *or* make it clear by the use of concrete examples

Interpret   expound the meaning of, make clear and explicit; usually giving your own judgment also

Justify   show adequate grounds for decisions or conclusions

Outline   give the main features or general principles of a subject, omitting minor details and emphasising structure and arrangement

Prove   demonstrate or establish the truth or accuracy of

Relate   *a* to narrate. More usually in examinations
b to show how things are connected to each other and to what extent they are alike, or affect each other

Review   to make a survey of, examining the subject critically

State   present in brief, clear form

Summarise   give a concise account of the chief points or substance of a matter, omitting details and examples

Trace   follow the development or history of a topic from some point or origin